Sand dunes, Death Valley, with Grapevine Mountains in background.

OUR CHANGING EARTH
THROUGH THE AGES

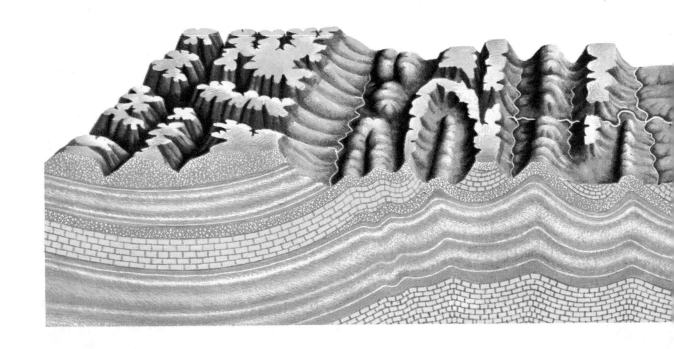

THE STORY OF
GEOLOGY

by Jerome Wyckoff

Illustrated with Photographs

and with Paintings by

William Sayles, Harry McNaught, and Raymond Perlman

REVISED EDITION

GOLDEN PRESS NEW YORK

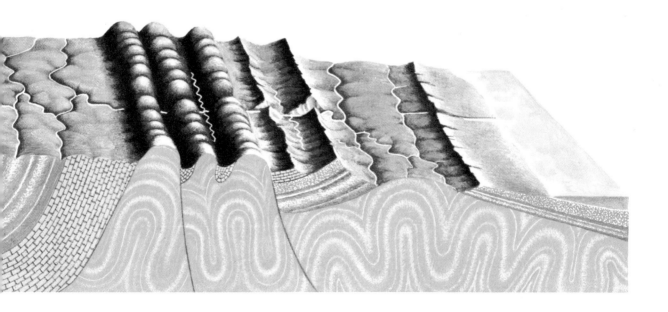

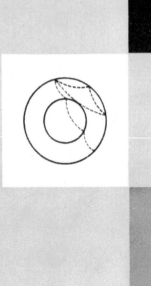

Library of Congress Catalog Card Number: 60-14878

CONTENTS

ACKNOWLEDGMENTS

The author and the publishers are indebted to Dr. Brian Mason, Curator of Physical Geology and Mineralogy, American Museum of Natural History, and to Dr. George Gaylord Simpson, Museum of Comparative Zoology, Harvard University, for professional advice generously given in regard to the text and illustrations. Thanks are due also to the Photo Library, U.S. Geological Survey, Denver; the American Geographical Society, New York; the National Park Service; and the National Aeronautics and Space Administration for aid in the search for photographs.

Maps on the following pages were prepared in part with the aid of material from various sources: Pages 72–73—*Geology of the Great Lakes* by Jack L. Hough, Univ. of Illinois Press, Urbana, Ill., 1958. Page 115—*Historical Geology* by Carl O. Dunbar, John Wiley and Sons, New York, 1960. Pages 152–157—Lamont-Doherty Geological Observatory, by permission of Bruce Heezen. Page 158—National Science Foundation. Pages 162–163—"The Breakup of Pangea," by Robert S. Dietz and John C. Holden, *Scientific American,* October 1970. Information for the diagram on page 137 (bottom) was provided by Esso.

The paintings by Raymond Perlman are from *Rocks and Minerals* by Zim and Shaffer, Golden Press, New York, 1957.

ART CREDITS

ENID KOTSCHNIG: 117b, 118t

HARRY McNAUGHT: cover, 4-5, 6-7, 12, 16, 18t, 22, 26-27, 32-33, 41b, 42b, 47b, 54b, 59t, 60, 66-67, 69t, 74, 75b, 84b, 104t, 111b, 112t, 118b, 121t, 152, 159, 160, 162-163, 168-169t

RAYMOND PERLMAN: 35t, 36t, 104b, 106b, 109, 111t, 140-141b, 144-145, 146, 150, 151t

WILLIAM SAYLES: 71, 72-73b, 80, 82t, 87, 90-91b, 94-95, 98t, 103, 110, 113t, 115, 126, 129, 133, 134t, 136, 137, 142, 149, 151b, 154t, 155, 158, 161, 172-173, 174

PHOTOGRAPH CREDITS

Front endpapers Josef Muench; 10-11 Carlos Elmer; 13 U.S. Geological Survey; 14 George Wolfson; 15 Jerome Wyckoff; 17 Steve McCutcheon; 18 Jerome Wyckoff; 19 Bob and Ira Spring; 20tl, 20br Jerome Wyckoff; 20br Barnum Brown; 21 Jerome Wyckoff; 23 Harold Wanless; 28-29 David Muench; 30 Idaho Dept. of Commerce (Josef Muench); 32 Philip D. Gendreau; 34, 35 Jerome Wyckoff; 36 Josef Muench; 37t Horace Bristol—FPG; 37b American Geographical Society; 38t F. H. Pough-American Museum of Natural History; 38b Univ. of New South Wales; 39 Jerome Wyckoff; 40 U.S. Navy-American Geographical Society; 42 U.S. Geological Survey; 43 Josef Muench; 44 Bob and Ira Spring; 45 Oregon State Highway Dept.; 46t Samuel P. Haberman; 46b Jerome Wyckoff; 47 Jack Breed—F.P.G.; 48-49 Josef Muench; 50t Josef Muench; 50b South Dakota Dept. of Highways; 51b Harold Wanless; 51t, 52 Jerome Wyckoff; 53t Ruth Pieroth; 53b Hubert Lowman; 54 National Park Service; 55t Josef Muench; 55bl Jerome Wyckoff; 55br San Francisco Chronicle—Bill Young; 56t State of Colorado; 56b William Maher; 57 State of Colorado; 58 Soil Conservation Comm., U.S. Dept. of Agriculture; 59 Jerome Wyckoff; 61t Josef Muench; 61b Jerome Wyckoff; 62t Laurence Lowry-Rapho Guillaumette; 62b Jerome Wyckoff; 63 B.A. Butt-Philip D. Gendreau; 64 Luray Caverns; 68 Jerome Wyckoff; 69 National Park Service; 70 Russ Kinne; 71 Jerome Wyckoff; 72 Bob and Ira Spring; 73 Ray Atkeson; 74 Laurence Lowry-Rapho Guillaumette; 75 Annan Photo Features; 76 Stephen Warner-Shostal; 77 Bob Taylor—F.P.G.; 78-79 Robert Bagby—F.P.G.; 81t Jerome Wyckoff; 81b Ruth Pieroth; 83, 84 Jerome Wyckoff; 85t National Park Service; 85b Russ Kinne; 86t Soil Conservation Comm.—U.S. Dept of Agriculture; 86-87 Freeport Sulphur Co.—FLO; 88 Jerome Wyckoff; 89t National Park Service; 89b, 90 Jerome Wyckoff; 91 Ruth Pieroth; 92-93 U.S. Navy-American Geographical Society; 94, 95 Josef Muench; 96 Jerome Wyckoff; 97t Josef Muench; 97b Jerome Wyckoff; 98 Dick Smith; 99 Jerome Wyckoff; 100 U.S. Geological Survey (Austin Post); 101 William O. Field-American Geographical Society; 102 South Dakota Dept. of Highways; 105, 106 Jerome Wyckoff; 107t National Park Service; 107b Jerome Wyckoff; 108 Canadian National Travel Bureau; 109, 112 Jerome Wyckoff; 113bl Ward's Natural Science Establishment; 113br Sinclair Oil Corp.; 114 Bob Ellis—F.P.G.; 116t Jerome Wyckoff; 116b Harold Wanless; 117, 119, 120, 121 Jerome Wyckoff; 122t State of Colorado; 122b Jerome Wyckoff; 123 Royal Canadian Air Force; 124-125, 127 David Muench; 128 State of Colorado; 130 Carlos Elmer; 131 Fritz Henle-Monkmeyer; 132 N.Y. Public Library; 135 U.P.I.; 138, 139, 140 Jerome Wyckoff; 142 Rock of Ages Corp.; 148 Anaconda; 154 Francis P. Shepard; 156-157t Lamont-Doherty Geological Observatory; 157b U.S. Coast and Geodetic Survey; 164, 165 NASA; 166 American Museum of Natural History; 167b Bob and Ira Spring; 168b, 170b American Museum of Natural History; 170t Ward's Natural Science Establishment; 171 Barnum Brown; 175 Utah Tourist and Publicity Agency; *back endpapers* Ed Ellinger-Shostal

FOREWORD

EARTH as we see it today is one frame of a moving picture that has been running for billions of years, and will run for billions of years more. Wherever we are, all around us, the ages-long story of erosion, of lands rising and falling, of volcanoes erupting and glaciers forming, of rocks and minerals being created, is in the making. Within one's own life span, the changes may seem infinitesimally small, but in geology a thousand years are as a day.

As an outdoor-minded people, we are becoming more aware of geological features around us. We travel thousands of miles to see the Grand Canyon and Yosemite, Niagara Falls and the Great Lakes, the Appalachian Mountains and the volcanoes of Mexico, the coasts of Cape Cod and Oregon. More and more of us become "rock hounds" and fossil hunters. Geology, the study of Earth's crust, becomes a fascinating story that he who travels can learn to read.

This is a book for people who like the feel of Earth underfoot, who want to know the meanings of landscapes and seascapes. But also it is a book that shows how the phenomena of Earth's crust influence our whole way of life. The bricks and cement for our houses and highways, the metals for our automobiles and appliances, the coal for our fuels and plastics, even the soil for our crops—all these are from the planet's crust. The stages of human history, from the Stone Age through the Copper and Bronze, to the Iron Age and now the Atomic Era, reflect man's increasing knowledge and use of mineral resources.

We are, every one of us, intimate parts of the world of the geologist.

This book ventures across the borders of such sciences as meteorology, the study of weather and climate; geophysics, which concentrates on Earth's interior; and paleontology, which deals with life of the past. But it is essentially the story of geology. I welcome this effort to tell it as living, exciting knowledge.

BRIAN MASON

Curator of Physical Geology and Mineralogy
American Museum of Natural History

Changing Earth

WHEN we look at a mountain or a desert, a valley or a sea, it seems that they must always have been as they are now. Man can cut down a forest or blast a hill away, but who can build a mountain range or set the boundaries of an ocean? No wonder people use such expressions as "the everlasting hills" and "the eternal sea."

Actually Earth is constantly being transformed. The process has been going on for several billion years and probably will go on for billions of years to come.

Some Earth changes are sudden and exciting. When a volcano blows its top, a great river floods over its banks, or an earthquake shakes the land—we take notice. But mostly the changes are slow. Five or ten thousand years to make a desert . . . a hundred thousand years to cut a small valley . . . ten million years to build a mountain range—that's how Earth uses time.

Think · of some ways in which Earth is at this moment changing:

All the mountains of the world are gradually being destroyed by the action of frost, gravity, and running water. Some day the highest mountains will be no more.

Sea bottoms in some regions are rising. Ages from now they may be snow-capped peaks.

There are places where the sea is creeping in over the land. In the far future, fish and crabs may swim where cities are today.

As recently as 15,000 years ago, ice sheets covered most of North America and northern Europe. The ice has since melted back to Greenland and other arctic regions. In another 10,000 years all Greenland could be as warm as Florida today.

The book of Earth—*The rock layers of Grand Canyon, here seen from Toroweap Point, record a billion years of Earth history. The Colorado River has taken about two million years to cut most of the canyon.*

AURORA

POLAR ICEFIELDS

ATMOSPHERE

ICE
SHEET

VOLCANOES

LANDS RISING AND SINKING

WEATHER

VARIETY OF ROCKS

GLACIERS

MOUNTAINS

MINERALS

LAKES

MODERATE
TEMPERATURES

SUBMARINE MOUNTAINS

VOLCANOES

VOLCANIC
ISLANDS

EROSION

DESERT

VOLCANIC
ISLANDS

VAST EXPANSES OF WATER

HEAVY VEGETATION

RIVER SYSTEMS

MOUNTAINS

EARTHQUAKES

VARIETY OF
LIVING THINGS

POLAR ICEFIELDS

An earth scientist's view of our planet—*With its abundant atmosphere, varied landscapes, plentiful water, and moderate temperatures, Earth is unique in the solar system.*

Earth's crust in the making—*Volcanic activity in many parts of the world continues to build up our planet's crust. This is Shishaldin Volcano, a composite cone in the Aleutian Islands.*

Does anyone suppose that there can be only one Grand Canyon in Earth's history? Somewhere a river has begun cutting a greater one.

As highlands wear down, their debris—clay, sand, stones—is washed and blown down onto lowlands or into the sea. These sediments, gradually turning to hard rock, may become miles thick—and may be raised to make mountains again.

In layers of sedimentary rock we find fossils —remains of animals and plants of ancient times. Organic remains of our time, too, are being buried in mud to become fossils ages hence.

Inland seas, such as the Great Lakes, have been where they are for thousands of years. But that is only a second on the geological clock. A few more seconds and the sparkling waters will be gone.

Deep in the planet is a domain of terrific heat and pressure. Here limestone is changed to marble, shale to slate, lava rock to schist. Earth's dark interior is a laboratory of change.

Here and there, Earth's crust bends, bulges, or breaks. White-hot material surges upward through cracks, is erupted through volcanoes, and cools to solid rock. Thus new crust is being built.

The enormous plates of rock that make up the crust are moving. Over millions of years these plates, carrying entire continents, travel thousands of miles.

Are you reading these words in a town or city? A hundred thousand years from now that place may be under a mile of ice—or it may be a warm swampland like the Florida Everglades. In a million years it may be a sea bottom. Twenty million years from today it may be a land of snowy mountains.

Such are the ways of changing Earth.

OUR REMARKABLE PLANET

Among all the planets of the solar system, Earth is very likely the most diversified, the most changeable, the most scenic.

Some other members of the Sun's family have atmospheres and, therefore, weather. But no other planet can match Earth's blue skies patched with clouds, flaming sunrises and sun-

13

Sculptors of Earth's surface—*Air and water, more than any other agents, shape the face of our planet and produce its scenery. This is Wyoming's Teton Range, with Jackson Lake in the foreground.*

sets, rainbows and blizzards, sleet storms and April showers.

No other planet can boast snow-capped mountains, sprawling glaciers, rushing rivers. Mars and Venus have deserts and dust storms mightier than the Sahara's, but only Earth shows sunlit lakes and landscapes of living green. The extremely hot, dry volcanic landscapes of Mercury and Venus must be forbidding and monotonous. Jupiter, Neptune, Uranus, and Pluto are wrapped in layers of frozen gases so thick that they could not possibly have landscapes anything like Earth's.

The cutting of valleys by rivers, the tunneling of the crust by ground water, the phenomena of springs and swamps—these events are happening nowhere in the solar system except here.

Earth's diversity of minerals, which depends partly on atmospheric action, is probably un-excelled. And only Earth possesses plentiful supplies of water—in liquid form thanks to our moderate temperatures. Liquid water is vital to all living things. More than any other agent, liquid water acts in both physical and chemical ways to keep the planet's surface changing.

Earth, as the only planet of the solar system that could support a large variety of living things, is a unique museum and a graveyard for the life of the past. On no other known planet do men read history in the rocks and contemplate vanished worlds.

THE SEA OF AIR

First among the agents at work on Earth is the atmosphere. At the bottom of the deep ocean of air live people, birds, and plants much as fish, oysters, and seaweeds live in the ocean of water. Wherever we go, on land or sea, we are in the atmosphere. We think no more about it than a fish thinks about swimming.

Air is made of molecules and atoms of gas, and of smaller atomic particles—all too tiny to see in a microscope. The atmosphere's weight at sea level is more than 14 pounds on every square inch of area. That's about one ton per square foot. On mountain heights the pressure is much less—about 5½ pounds, for example, on Mount Everest. At least three fourths of all the atmosphere is packed into the layer within ten miles of the ground.

This air blanket around Earth is constantly shifting. Rays from the Sun keep shooting down into it. Striking the air and dust particles, and the ground itself, these rays produce heat, just as sunlight pouring into a greenhouse makes heat there. Heat makes the air particles move faster and get farther apart. Thus heated air is lighter and tends to rise above cooler, heavier air. In this way winds are started.

The atmosphere is disturbed also by the gravitational attraction of Moon and Sun, and by Earth's rotation. As Earth turns, it tends to drag the atmosphere along with it, because of the friction between air and ground. Thus directions of winds are affected.

As the air moves over water and land, it picks up moisture in the form of tiny particles called water vapor. These particles float between the particles of air. The warmer the air is, the wider the spaces between the air particles and the more water particles it has room for.

Moist air moves over Earth's surface and works down into the crust. It attacks the rock, gradually changing it chemically and breaking it up. This process is called weathering.

Water from rain or melting snow trickles down into cracks in solid rock. If the water freezes, it expands and breaks the rock. Much of our planet is covered with rock broken up by freezing action—another kind of weathering.

Weathering and mass wasting—*Water freezing in crevices in this mountain cliff breaks off pieces of rock. These fall, forming heaps of talus below.*

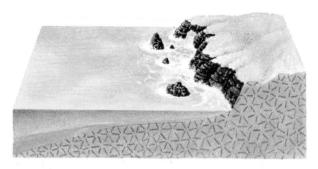

Erosion of Coasts by Waves and Currents

Carving of Landscapes by Running Water

Shaping of Lands by Glacier Ice

Underground Tunneling by Ground Water

Deposit of Rock Waste in Basins

Broken, loosened rock is pulled down by gravity. Rock fragments fall from cliffs, tumble down hillsides, or slide bit by bit down gentle slopes. Large masses of this material may descend as rockslides or mudflows. Downslope movements are known as mass wasting.

RUNNING WATER SHAPES THE LAND

Suppose a warm, dry wind from the land blows over the sea. It picks up billions of water particles. Then it moves over a cooler area. The air becomes chilled and can no longer hold so much water. In the process called condensation, some of the water changes into small visible drops, which often form around bits of dust. Large, dense groups of these droplets are seen by us as clouds, and from these rain or snow may fall. On land, some of the water sinks underground, some is captured by roots of plants, a little is used by animals and people, and much is evaporated into the air again. But about a fourth of it drains back toward the sea by way of streams.

Streams move over land by gravity. They carry along clay, sand, pebbles, and larger pieces of rock, which scrape the bottoms and sides of the stream channels. Thus, with help from weathering and mass wasting on their banks, streams keep widening and deepening their valleys. Most of the world's valleys have been carved by this process of downcutting by streams—"stream erosion"—aided by weathering and mass wasting.

Some streams flow underground. There they may dissolve rock to make tunnels and caverns.

On very cold lands, the snow of many winters may build up to depths of hundreds of feet. Gradually the snow turns to great masses of ice called glaciers. Glacier ice grinds down through mountain valleys, deepening and widening them.

Through the ages, rock waste is carried by streams from highlands down onto lowlands. Where the flowing water slows down, it deposits some of this rock waste, which is called alluvium. Alluvium forms fans, floodplains, and deltas. Some alluvium eventually is carried to the sea.

A river of ice—*Ruth Glacier, on Alaska's Mt. McKinley, is a reminder of ages past during which ice sheets covered lands now inhabited by man.*

A SEA WITH ISLANDS

Earth as seen by astronauts in space is a sphere covered partly by swirling clouds. Through openings in the clouds there are glimpses of the blue world ocean, patched with large "islands"—actually, the continents. Water dominates the scene. No less than 70 per cent of the planet is covered by ocean water.

The world ocean contains something like 330 million cubic miles of water. If Earth were a perfect sphere with a smooth surface, sea water would cover it to a depth of a mile and a half. The depth of the oceans can be compared to a film a hundredth of an inch thick over a desk globe 35 inches in diameter.

The sea is in unending motion. Currents are caused by Earth's rotation, by river water pouring into the sea, by differences in temperatures or salt content of the water. The pull of Sun and Moon keeps great bulges of water—"tides"—moving around the planet. Wind blowing over water makes waves, most of them small but some—the great storm waves—as high as 75 feet from trough to crest.

The sea works against the land. Ocean waves and currents chew away at the edges of conti-nents. Currents help to shape ocean bottoms, particularly near the continents.

Along some edges of continents are gently sloping, sea-covered "shelves." As Earth's crust heaves up and down through the millennia, these shelves become dry land, then sea bottom, then dry land again, at various times. Even the interiors of the continents are invaded now and then by sea water.

On deep ocean bottoms, where light never penetrates, are vast plains covered with the ooze of millions of years, mixed with rust of innumerable meteorites that have hit the planet through the ages. These plains are dotted with submarine volcanoes and divided by long undersea mountain ranges. Some peaks rise above the waves as islands, such as the Hawaiian and Canary Islands. Deep clefts called trenches split the ocean bottoms, reaching four to seven miles below sea level. Trenches are centers of earthquake activity.

In the salty green world of the sea, crossed by currents like lazy winds, communities of plants and animals are as busy and varied as any on land. Some of these living things, such as the corals and foraminifers, are builders of

17

The crust of Earth—*This cross section illustrates the relationship of ocean bottoms, continental masses (mostly granitic), and underlying rock (mainly basaltic). Vertical scale is exaggerated to show details more clearly.*

reefs, islands, and bottom deposits of limestone. These tiny organisms, too, have a part in making Earth's crust and changing its face.

THE ANATOMY OF THE CRUST

The crust is the outermost layer of the planet, except for the atmosphere. Wherever we may be—in forest, desert, city, swamp, or ocean—below us lies this hard layer. It is made of "bedrock." Patches of broken rock, soil, and water lie on the crust here and there.

Bedrock is the solid stone we see exposed on mountain tops, in roadcuts, in quarries. Vast masses of bedrock often are visible in the sides of valleys with very steep sides, such as the Grand Canyon. Bedrock is always somewhat fractured, or cracked. It may be in layers, blocks, sheets, columns, or domes. It comes in all colors.

Parts of the crust have been folded, broken, or tilted. Great blocks and folds have risen to form mountains or sunk to make lowlands.

ROCK VARIETIES

Bedrock is made up of minerals—hundreds of kinds—that have formed by combinations of the basic elements of nature. For example, quartz sandstone is made mainly of quartz grains. Quartz is made of the elements silicon and oxygen. Most limestone consists mainly of the mineral calcite, made of calcium, carbon, and oxygen.

Bedrocks are of three broad classes. First are the igneous rocks—those formed by cooling of molten material coming up from Earth's interior. Cooled lava and granite are examples.

Next are the sedimentary rocks. Some, such as sandstone and shale, formed from crumbled

Igneous rock—*A lava flow of the basalt type cooled to form these columns near Coulee Dam, Washington.*

Sedimentary rock—*Layers of shale and limestone alternate with coal in roadcut in western Pennsylvania.*

Metamorphic rock—*An outcrop of gneiss in New York's Hudson Highlands with an S-fold due to pressure.*

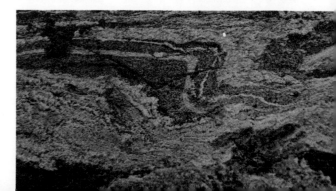

rock material. Others, such as some kinds of limestone, are made of limy remains of organisms such as corals. Still others, like salt, form by evaporation of water from solutions.

Finally there are the metamorphic rocks. These consist of igneous or sedimentary rock changed by heat, pressure, or liquids or gases infiltrating them. Marble, gneiss, and schist are examples of rocks in this class. Others are quartzite and slate.

Earth's crust can be imagined as a shell of igneous rock, covered with a thin layer of sedimentary and metamorphic rocks. The ocean bottom is of igneous rock, with a thin blanket of sediments. The continents mostly have a thick cover of sedimentary and metamorphic rocks which, in places, thin to show the underlying igneous rock.

Bedrock of all kinds is still being made as it has been made through ages. Here and there, molten material called magma rises from Earth's interior through fractures and cools either within the crust or on the surface to make new igneous rock. Sedimentary rock is being created where sediments are packed down by the weight of sediments above them and are cemented by mineral-bearing waters percolating through them. Both igneous and sedimentary rocks are now, as in the past, being converted into metamorphic rock.

As bedrocks form, new supplies of minerals are added to Earth's unique and varied stock. However, useful minerals are not being made by nature as fast as man is using them up.

Layers of soil cover most bedrock. All soils consist of rock that has been crumbled and changed chemically, and mixed with decayed remains of plants and animals.

Much soil eventually becomes sedimentary rock, such as sandstone or shale. This may be converted to metamorphic rock, like quartzite or slate. Or it may be melted and cooled again to make igneous rock. Thus Earth recycles its rock materials over and over.

The ever-working sea—*Seashores, through the ages, are being cut back by attacks of waves and currents. But uplifting forces in Earth's crust tend to keep continental surfaces above water. This is Ecola State Park, Oregon.*

A relic of ancient life—*A fossil fish imprint, 50 million years old, was exposed when this piece of shale from Wyoming was split off a larger slab.*

TRACES OF THE PAST

In sedimentary rock geologists find clues to Earth's past and to the plant and animal species that lived on the planet long ago. Bony parts, carbon remains, and casts or imprints of once-living things may be preserved in rock for millions of years. Then they are revealed as the rock erodes away or as slabs or flakes break off.

Remains or traces of ancient life are called fossils. Found in sedimentary rocks all over the world, they enable geologists to piece together the marvelous story of life from very early times.

Some kinds of bedrock contain natural "clocks." These are bits of chemical elements that are radioactive. Gradually such substances break down to form stable elements. Since the rate of breakdown for each radioactive element is known, tests can show how much time has passed since the rock formed. In this way the ages of bedrocks in various parts of the world have been determined. Where the age of bedrock is known, the age of fossils in that rock also is known. With such knowledge, scientists can tell much about the past history of Earth and its living things.

A scientific "grave robber"—*This paleontologist, exploring a rich dinosaur fossil bed in the Montana badlands, finds clues to the world of 100 million years ago.*

"Frozen" dunes—*Hillocks of sandstone in Zion National Park, Utah, are remains of ancient desert dunes cemented by ground water. Note the crossbedded layers.*

THE MYSTERIOUS DEPTHS

The crust is only two to eight miles thick beneath the trenches in the ocean bottoms, but 30 to 35 miles thick beneath the higher parts of the continents. The deepest mines—the gold mines of South Africa—reach down less than two miles, and the deepest oil wells less than five. The center of the planet is nearly 4,000 miles deeper than that.

The deeper bedrock is, the greater is the weight on it. Ten miles down, the weight is about 4,600 tons per square foot. That compares to a weight of 16 tons—the weight of five average automobiles—on a single dime.

Beneath the crust is the mantle, a layer of heavy, somewhat rocklike material about 1,800 miles thick. Here temperatures may be around 5,000 degrees Fahrenheit, and the pressure over one million times the pressure of the atmosphere at sea level. That would be equal to about 40,000 tons on the dime.

Under such awesome pressure the mantle rock (if it can be called rock) behaves plastically. A disturbance in the mantle can make it bend, twist, or flow like bread dough. A de-

Strongly deformed rock—*A roadcut in California's San Gabriel Mountains shows layers of schist folded, broken, and dislocated by deep earth forces.*

New rock from the depths—*Volcanic cones and fields of basalt lava about 900 years old are seen in the vicinity of Sunset Crater north of Flagstaff, Arizona. In the foreground, vegetation is growing on the rough aa lava.*

crease in pressure can cause it to melt. It is in the mantle that the severest earthquakes are known to originate.

Under the mantle is a region called the outer core. This may consist of nickel or iron, in liquid form because of the great heat. The outer core, perhaps 1,300 miles thick, surrounds the inner core, at the planet's center. The inner core is believed to be a more nearly rigid ball of iron and nickel about 1,600 miles in diameter. The ball may be so squeezed that it has shrunk, taking up less space than it would aboveground. The pressure on it may be four million times the pressure of the atmosphere at sea level.

In the mantle and in the core scientists find clues to Earth's magnetism. Here may lie explanations for shifts in Earth's magnetic field and in locations of the north and south magnetic poles. What happens in the mantle influences the gradual drifting of the plates that make up the crust.

We usually think of planet Earth as being very hard and solid. We might better compare it to a much-cracked fresh egg about ready to fall apart. Our planet is held together by its own gravitational attraction: all parts are subject to a pull toward the center. If a large celestial body like Jupiter or the Sun passed near us, its gravity would pull Earth to pieces.

Inside Earth—*A cutaway view shows the comparatively thin crust, thick mantle, and outer and inner cores. These structures are inferred from the behavior of seismic waves that travel through the planet (see page 137).*

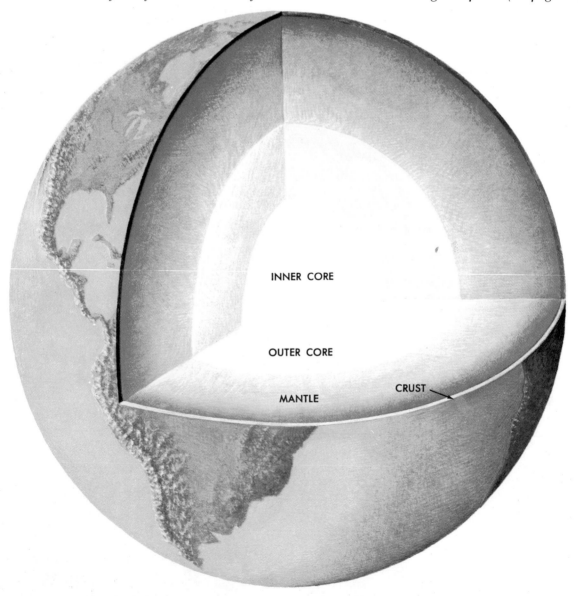

INNER CORE

OUTER CORE

MANTLE

CRUST

RESTLESS ROCK

Mostly, Earth's crust seems quiet, but forces are ever at work to disturb it.

As the land erodes, millions of tons of rock waste move down to lower areas. There the waste may pile up so thickly that the crust bends beneath it. Meanwhile the crust may rise where much rock has been removed.

Other disturbances of the crust are caused by the pull of Sun and Moon, and by heat produced in the crust by radioactivity. This heat can cause the crust to swell, crack, or shift. Magma may burst forth to form volcanoes.

The mantle, beneath the crust, contains radioactive material and is very hot and mobile. Mantle material rises from the core toward the underside of the crust, cools a little as it moves horizontally, then turns down again. These convection currents, perhaps like the currents of air around a radiator, probably disturb the crust, causing various movements.

It is in the ocean floors that crustal activity is most evident. Molten material from the mantle comes up through rifts between the great plates that make up the crust. The molten matter spreads out, cooling to make new crust. The plates move; and where they collide, one descends below the other into the mantle.

Most mountain ranges are built up by plate movements. Colliding plates crumple in some places to make what are known as fold mountains. Blocks may shift up and down to make a landscape of "block mountains" and valleys.

Most crustal movements are slight jumps of only a fraction of an inch. Such movements occur frequently in all parts of the world, but go unnoticed by most of us. In some areas there are occasional movements of a few feet or more, with earthquakes severe enough to do much damage and kill many people.

Balancing movements tend to leave lighter blocks of the crust standing higher than the heavier ones. The upper parts of lighter blocks reach above sea level; the largest form continents. The top surfaces of heavier blocks are the ocean bottoms.

Crustal movements continue today as in the past. Truly, we live on a changing Earth.

A fold in Earth's restless crust—*Mt. Timpanogos, in northeastern Utah, testifies to the ancient collision of crustal plates that buckled the crust into great folds and made the Rocky Mountains.*

Where Earth's crust broke—*Here faulting has dislocated sandstone strata of different colors. In the fault at right, note the dragging effect of the displacement on the layers.*

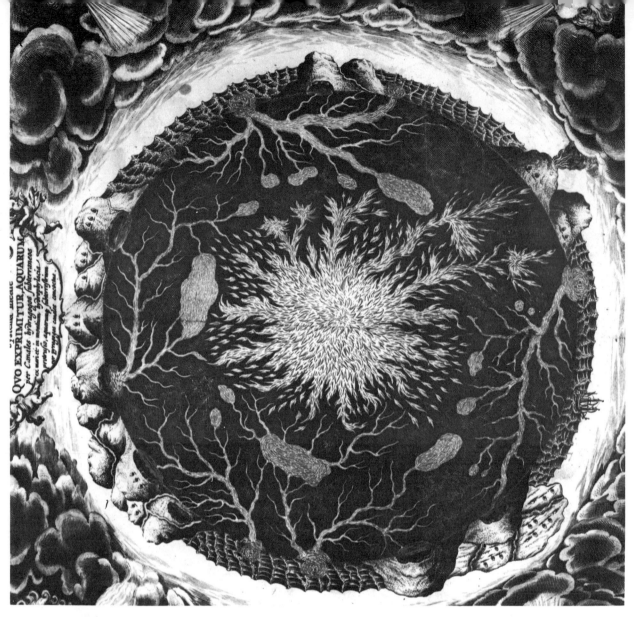

Earth's interior: a 17th-century view—*This drawing in Kircher's* Mundus Subterraneus *("The Underground World," 1664) shows a great fire at Earth's center, vast caverns, the roots of volcanoes, and branching channels through which water descends from sea bottoms and rises up into mountains. Kircher was a leading thinker of his time.*

Reading the Rocks

UNTIL about two centuries ago, even people of wide knowledge had little inkling of how the "natural" world was created and has been changed since. Geological events were commonly regarded as works of God. God was unpredictable; his works were mysterious—and not to be studied too closely.

Today most people recognize the grand patterns of geologic change as natural. Events on Earth are seen as works of nature, even if nature is believed to have a divine being behind it. But this twentieth-century understanding of natural processes did not come easily. It came from long, patient observation and careful reasoning. It came with the scientific approach to knowledge.

In ancient times there was no shortage of thinkers who asked How? and Why? and By what? Most of their thinking was about religious matters, but some were curious about common things like mountains and rocks, volcanoes and earthquakes, fossils and rivers.

The Greek thinker Ptolemy reasoned that Earth must be a ball, with a gigantic fire inside. The famed Greek philosopher Aristotle believed that rock is formed from effects of sunlight and starlight on the crust. He taught that earthquakes and volcanoes result from violent winds underground. The ideas of this world-famous teacher reigned over civilization for two thousand years.

As recently as a few hundred years ago, most learned people believed Earth to be flat. They said mountains were raised up by the "pull" of starlight. (Mountains do seem to reach toward the stars!) They suspected that fossils are the secret writings of spirits in the rocks. Whole books were written to describe how minerals form in the bodies—so scholars said—of animals and plants. River waters, the philosophers thought, run down to the ocean, leak through holes in the bottom, flow underground up into the mountains, and then pour down over the land to the ocean again.

Thinkers of those days were as intelligent as we are. But they had little solid knowledge to work with. Many of their "facts" had been thought up—invented out of nothing. They did not know that careful observation, plus systematic reasoning, is the road to knowledge.

ANSWERS IN THE ROCKS

A few hundred years ago some thinkers were looking at the world in a new way. They were trying to trace out a world of natural causes and effects.

In Poland, Nicholas Copernicus carefully recorded the changing positions of Sun, Moon, planets, and stars. Before he died, in 1543, he declared that Earth revolves around the Sun, not the Sun around Earth.

In 1609 Galileo Galilei, the great Italian experimenter, made himself a small telescope, used it to explore the heavens, and decided Copernicus was right. In the same year Johannes

Anatomy of a volcano—*Kircher's* Mundus Subterraneus *shows a great fire beneath erupting Mt. Vesuvius.*

Kepler, the German astronomer, came forward with formulas to explain the orbits of planets around the Sun. Late in the century, England's Isaac Newton was studying gravity and the laws of motion.

By the middle 1700s, certain thinkers were carefully observing Earth's crust just as others

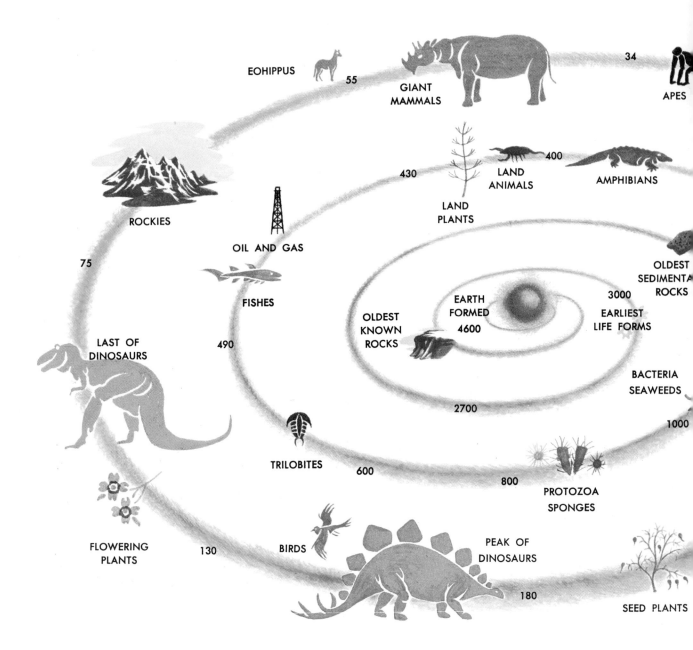

EOHIPPUS 55

GIANT MAMMALS

34

APES

430 LAND PLANTS

LAND ANIMALS

400

AMPHIBIANS

ROCKIES

OIL AND GAS

EARTH FORMED 4600

OLDEST SEDIMENTARY ROCKS

3000

EARLIEST LIFE FORMS

75

FISHES

OLDEST KNOWN ROCKS

BACTERIA SEAWEEDS

1000

LAST OF DINOSAURS

490

2700

TRILOBITES 600

800

PROTOZOA SPONGES

FLOWERING PLANTS

130

BIRDS

PEAK OF DINOSAURS

180

SEED PLANTS

had studied the heavens. They, too, were beginning to trace out natural causes and effects.
And they began to glimpse answers to some
baffling old questions.

It was noticed that some regions are covered
with bedrocks that obviously were once molten
—so hot that they flowed. Could it be that our
planet's surface had been formed in fire?

Some observers saw how frost action forces
rocks apart, how moist air decays rock surfaces,
how running water carves gullies in hillsides
and fields. Could it be that whole valleys have
been carved—whole mountains sculptured—by
air and water through long ages?

Over some regions lie thick layers of rock
that look somewhat like the hardened layers of
clay or sand seen on bottoms of dried-up lakes
and rivers. Could these layered bedrocks be
hardened masses of rock particles and other
wastes laid down through centuries by rivers,
lakes, and seas?

In rocks of some high mountains—the Himalayas, the Alps, the Rockies—are fossils of fish,
seaweeds, and other things that surely at some
time lived in an ocean. Were sea bottoms somehow raised to become mountain ranges?

Fossils were thought by some naturalists to
be the remains of very ancient living things.

26

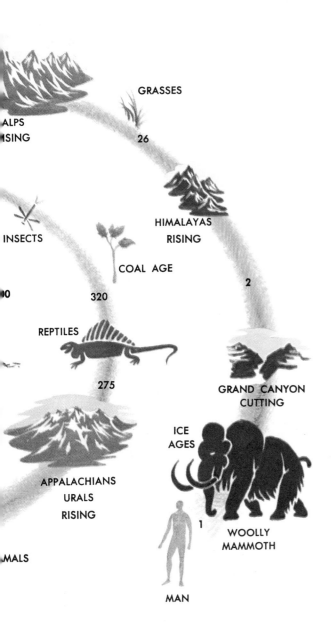

GRASSES

ALPS
RISING

26

INSECTS

HIMALAYAS
RISING

COAL AGE

2

0

320

REPTILES

275

GRAND CANYON
CUTTING

ICE
AGES

APPALACHIANS
URALS
RISING

1

WOOLLY
MAMMOTH

MALS

MAN

The spiral of time—*Earth history begins with the birth of the solar system (center of spiral). Numbers indicate millions of years ago. If the 6,000 years of human history were shown by just one inch of the spiral, the spiral if in scale would be 15 miles long.*

What stories could these strange relics tell of life in the distant past?

THE BIRTH OF GEOLOGY

With such questions began the scientific study of Earth—the science of geology. Like other sciences it grew rapidly during the nineteenth century. Alert, curious men tramped over Europe and the British Isles, North America, Africa, and South America, the oceanic islands and Asia, reading the rocks as they went. They looked, measured, compared. Facts were put together like pieces of a jigsaw puzzle. Gradually, as that puzzle took shape, it became a vast panorama of Earth change during the long, long past.

There were, of course, baffling questions, and perhaps the most important was the question of time. Early geologists were coming to believe Earth has been shaped by natural processes— earth movements, erosion, and volcanic activity. But most natural processes are slow. It was hard to believe the world we see today is old enough to have been shaped by geologic processes alone.

In ancient Babylonia, four thousand years ago, priests had imagined Earth as created out of chaos two million years before. A lot could happen in that length of time. But scholars of two centuries ago, studying ancient history and the Bible, considered Earth to be much younger. Ten thousand years, possibly fifty thousand, seemed the utter limit. But could whole mountain ranges be raised up and worn down, could mile-deep bedrocks be formed, could valleys be cut thousands of feet deep into rock—in fifty thousand years?

Such were the doubts. But during the early 1800s the truth was gradually revealed. Evidence indicated an enormous age for the world.

There were the layers of sedimentary rock, many thousands of feet thick. Geologists observed the deposition of sediments by streams and wind on land, and from water on lake and shallow sea bottoms. If the rates of deposition had been about the same through Earth history, millions of years would have been required to build up the sedimentary rocks. If, for example, the rate of formation of limestone on an ocean bottom was taken as a few inches per thousand years (that seemed a reasonable estimate), a 1,000-foot deposit would represent three million years of deposition.

Geologists climbed mountains, measured folded rock layers, and estimated how much of the layers had been eroded away. They estimated present rates of erosion and calculated

27

how long it would take for mountains to be eroded down to sea level. The answer seemed to be—many millions of years.

Some geologists estimated the total amount of salt in the ocean. This salt was known to have been dissolved out of the land and poured into the ocean by rivers through the ages. How long had this process taken? The answer seemed to be—75 million years at least.

The concept of evolution, too, pointed to an enormous age for Earth. According to Charles Darwin and his followers, living things developed from simple one-celled organisms to the marvelously complicated mammals we call man. But evolution was known to be very slow among the higher living things. During all written history there had been little noticeable change in man or other mammals. Scientists decided that if higher forms actually have evolved from simpler ones, this process too—like the formation of sedimentary rocks—must have required millions of years.

As the twentieth century opened, many scientists had decided that the planet's age must be something like 100 million years. But their measuring methods had been inexact. By mid-century the more reliable method of radioactivity testing had been developed by nuclear physicists. This indicated at first an age of nearly two billion years for the oldest rocks so far discovered.

Meanwhile yet another group of scientists stepped forward: the astronomers. They had been using the giant new telescopes to observe physical changes in the Sun and other stars. They asserted that Earth and the other planets had developed surely some billions of years ago from eddies in a cloud of dust and gas revolving around the Sun. Some meteorites, the astronomers said, must be "leftovers" from the early days of the solar system. The age of the oldest meteorite, as tested by its radioactivity, was 4.6 billion years.

So, at last, it was revealed that Earth is indeed very old—much older than the early ge-

ologists thought. Truly, the secret of Earth, so long hidden from man, is time.

THE RUIN OF FORMER WORLDS

We live amid the ruin of former worlds—the wrecks of ancient landscapes and seascapes, of mountains and meadows and shores. Earth's crust is the graveyard of all the living things of the past and the remains of their dwelling places on land and in the sea.

Such magnificent spectacles as the Grand Canyon of the Colorado and the Big Badlands of South Dakota are easy to recognize as "ruins." But the rounded old granite hills of

The "wreck" of a former world—*Arizona's Monument Valley, like many other landscapes of our planet, is the ruin of an earlier landscape.*

Vermont, the rolling land of Ohio, the wheat-clad plains of Kansas, the duned beaches of Florida, the towering Rockies—these too are the ruins of former worlds.

These worlds are almost unimaginably remote in time. A few comparisons will show *how* remote:

The Colorado River has taken several million years to cut most of the Grand Canyon. The cut is at least as old as the very first apelike beings that could be called man's ancestors. The canyon is one hundred fifty times as old as the paintings by prehistoric man in the caves of France and Spain.

The Appalachian Mountains rose up about 250 million years ago. They are about forty thousand times as old as the Pyramids of Egypt.

The dinosaurs were at their peak about 100 million years ago. That is ten thousand times as long ago as the close of the Pleistocene, the most recent ice age.

Imagine a limestone forming on an ocean bottom at the rate of 4 inches per thousand years. In the twenty centuries of the Christian calendar only 8 inches of that limestone has formed.

This is how, as we read the rocks, we can begin to think of geologic time.

The Zone of Heat

Fire has been ever fascinating, often terrifying, to man. For perhaps a million years man has been gazing into campfires, watching the magic of burning, fleeing before forest fires. No natural phenomenon on Earth is watched with greater interest, not to say fear, than the eruption of a volcano. It is no wonder that primitive peoples and ancient philosophers believed the world to have been born in fire.

Today we know Earth did not start in a great fire. At no time has "fire" made or shaped any important part of our planet. It is true, however, that heat within the planet has greatly influenced the making and shaping of the crust. How the founders of geology reached this understanding makes a story worth telling.

NEPTUNISTS AND PLUTONISTS

Two centuries ago, early geologists were rejecting old ideas about Earth's creation. They were developing ideas based on personal observations. It was not enough for them to know that "God made the world." They wanted to know how—what natural forces were involved, how these forces worked, and how long it had taken. For clues they were studying all sorts of Earth phenomena, including earthquakes, volcanoes, floods, erosion, fossils, the ocean, bedrocks, and wind.

Soon after 1800 a bitter argument was raging among scientifically minded men about how bedrocks had formed. On one side were the Neptunists, named after the sea god Neptune because they believed all or nearly all bedrocks had formed underwater. Opposing them were the Plutonists, named after Pluto, god of the underworld and ruler of Earth's internal fires. The Plutonists insisted that basalt, granite, and some other bedrocks, called "sedi-

mentary" by the Neptunists, had originally been molten.

The Neptunists were led by Abraham Gottlob Werner, a famous teacher at the mining academy in Freiburg, Germany. They pointed impatiently at sandstones, shales, and limestones. Did not many of these layers contain shellfish—proof that they had been formed in water? Well, then, if basalt, granite, gneiss, and other bedrocks are often found *between* sedimentary

Where Earth erupted—*The Craters of the Moon area in Idaho was volcanically active only 500 years ago. In the foreground are spatter cones, formed by eruptions of volcanic gases. Beyond are extinct cinder cones.*

layers, these rocks too must be sedimentary—formed in water. In fact, according to Werner's teachings, Earth began as a sphere covered entirely by a muddy ocean. With time, the sediments gradually dropped to the bottom, accumulated in thick layers, and hardened to become the bedrocks.

Werner's beliefs seemed to have support from the Bible. Noah's Flood apparently explained not only the forming of rock underwater but the rumpling and cracking of rock layers. (What a violent flood it must have been!) Fossils were believed to be remains of plants and animals trapped in mud as the floodwaters dried up.

The Plutonists stuck to their belief that volcanic activity had produced basalt, granite, and certain other bedrocks. As early as 1752 the French naturalist Jean Guettard had noticed basalt among lavas in the Auvergne hills of

Did the builder know?—*The 11th-century chapel St. Michel d'Aiguille at Le Puy, France, was built 290 feet high on a volcanic neck. "Necks" were favored sites for churches and castles.*

A "FIERY" HISTORY

For years the argument raged. Werner never gave in, but gradually his supporters left him. His most brilliant student, Leopold von Buch, took one good look at the Auvergne basalt and joined the Plutonists. Werner never went to see for himself.

Von Buch, a man of tremendous curiosity, became the first great authority on volcanic activity. He showed that volcanoes do not result from the burning of coal, pitch, or other combustible substances underground, but are formed by molten material—far hotter than burning coal—coming up from the depths.

Von Buch and other Plutonists told the people of Europe that many of the quiet landscapes around them had formed from red-hot lava. The green-clad, domelike hills were old volcanoes, worn and gentled by time. In some places where no such hills are seen, lava had simply poured out of big cracks in the earth and spread over the land. In other places molten rock had cooled and hardened underground and later had been uncovered by erosion. Almost *any* place might at some time have been the scene of volcanic activity. What had happened once could happen again!

southern France. Later Nicolas Desmarest studied these basalt masses and found they were parts of the flows and therefore formerly molten. Similar basalt, said the Plutonists, exists in Germany, England, Ireland, and Scotland, and so these too must be old volcanic regions. In fact, large areas of Earth must at some time have blazed with volcanoes!

A volcanic region—*Igneous activity in the crust produces many landscape features, including volcanic cones, lava flows, dikes and sills, laccoliths, geysers and hot springs, and fumaroles.*

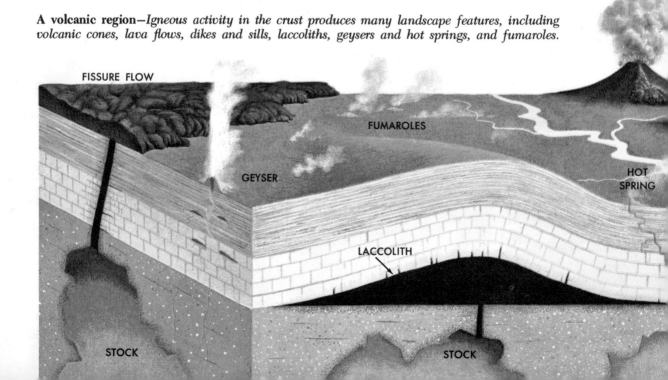

FISSURE FLOW

FUMAROLES

GEYSER

HOT SPRING

LACCOLITH

STOCK

STOCK

Some people were terrified. But in time their fears quieted. Geologists learned that most volcanic hills and mountains are harmless; they will not erupt again. They were active during relatively short intervals in the long geologic past. People could be reassured that new volcanic outbursts in places such as France, Scot-[land and] Ireland were virtually impossible,

volcanic past
science of ge-
lten rocks and
anding of how
rces that cause
and bend, fold,
piece to fit into
was created and

AGMA
are quantities of
ng periods these
erals, and in this
dditional heat re-
s. Still more is
rape against each
crust the heat is
forming what is
ccumulate under-

antle—under great
eat, too, probably

results partly from radioactivity. Being very hot and under great pressure, the mantle material can flow like a thick liquid. Where the crust is fractured all the way down to the mantle, the mantle material squeezes up into the fractures.

MAGMA THAT COOLS UNDERGROUND

Some magma solidifies underground to form masses of igneous rock called "plutons." Magma formed by melting within the crust cools to make light-colored rocks such as granite—rich

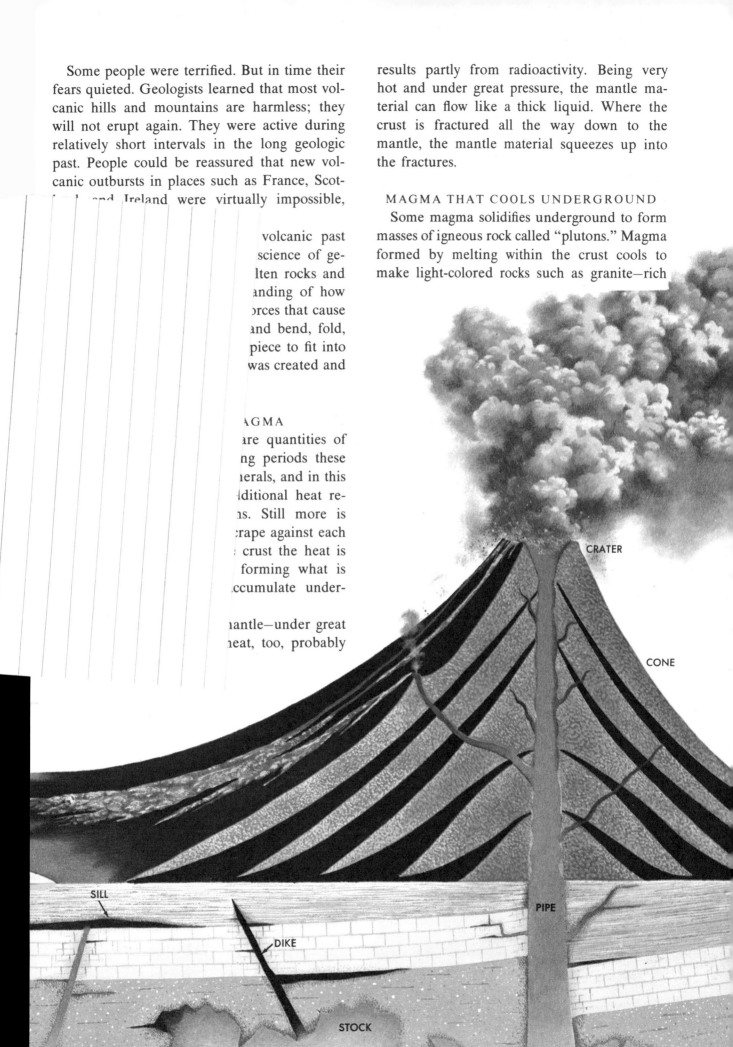

Dike and sill—*Granite injected into this mass of gneiss broke through and between horizontal layers to form a vertical dike and a horizontal sill.*

in feldspar and quartz—or syenite, which is nearly all feldspar. Magma coming from the lower crust or mantle cools to make darker "basaltic" rocks such as diabase or peridotite, which are rich in iron and magnesium.

Some magma freezes in various forms before it reaches the surface. Later, erosion may uncover it.

Magma forcing its way between rock layers may cool as a sheet or slab called a sill. The eastern edge of a sill forms the 20-mile-long scenic Palisades along the west side of the Hudson River northwest of New York City. For many millions of years erosion has been wearing away the soft red sandstone that once covered the sill entirely.

The Great Whin Sill of northern England is another such feature. It appears between northern Northumberland and the Farne Islands, then runs southwest, and finally turns southeast along the west side of the Pennine Hills.

An eroded laccolith—*Packsaddle Mountain, in Texas, shows remnants of limestone layers that covered it.*

When magma breaks *through* rock layers, rather than squeezing between them, it forms a dike. Dikes are common in volcanic regions. Upright dikes formed in softer rock become ridges as this rock is eroded away. Examples are the dikes running out from Ship Rock in New Mexico. Upright dikes in harder rock may be eroded out, leaving clefts or trenches in this harder rock. The famous Flume in New Hampshire's White Mountains is an example.

As magma forces its way between rock layers near the surface, the upper layers may bulge upward. The magma, cooling, becomes what is called a laccolith. Some laccoliths are large enough so that when erosion has removed softer rock covering them, they loom as mountains. Examples include the Highwood Mountains of Montana, the Abajos of Utah, several small peaks northwest of South Dakota's Black Hills, Packsaddle Mountain in the Texas Big Bend country, and Carrizo Peak in New Mexico.

Deep in the earth near fold mountain ranges there are likely to be large reservoirs of magma called stocks. These are the sources of lava for volcanoes, and of magma for dikes, sills, and other underground igneous intrusions. "Frozen" stocks uncovered by erosion become hills or mountains if the rock of the stock is more resistant than surrounding rock. The Henry Mountains of Utah and the Judith and Crazy Mountains of Montana are examples of stocks uncovered by erosion.

The largest underground magma reservoirs —great bodies more than 40 miles in diameter— are called batholiths (from the Greek words meaning "deep" and "rock"). They consist always of granite-like rock. Some batholiths have been raised as blocks from deep in the crust. Other batholiths are cores of fold mountain ranges—cores exposed by millions of years of erosion. Portions of the rock may consist of shale or sandstone that melted as the mountains were being pushed up.

In Idaho a vast batholith is exposed over an area of 16,000 square miles. Larger is the Coast Mountains batholith of western Canada and Alaska, 1,200 miles long and 80 to 120 miles wide. The Black Hills of South Dakota have been carved from a smaller batholith.

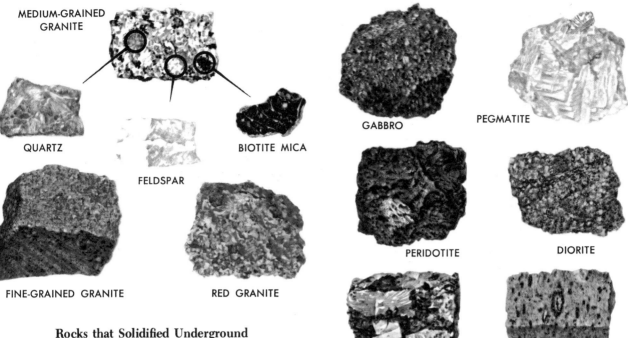

MEDIUM-GRAINED
GRANITE

QUARTZ

FELDSPAR

BIOTITE MICA

FINE-GRAINED GRANITE

RED GRANITE

GABBRO

PEGMATITE

PERIDOTITE

DIORITE

GRANITE PORPHYRY

SYENITE

Rocks that Solidified Underground

A VOLCANO IS BUILT

The bursting of magma through the crust into the outer world is called volcanic activity. Often this results in the building of a volcano.

Magma rising up through the crust is very hot —as high as 1,800 degrees Fahrenheit. Highly charged with gases, it can dissolve rock and even metals. It may break off chunks of rock in the fracture through which it is moving. When it meets underground water, the water is changed into steam.

As magma rises, the weight pressing on it from above lessens, allowing parts of the magma to turn to gases. These expand as the pressure from above continues to decrease. Thus they make the magma foam like soda pop as it nears the volcanic vent—the opening through which it emerges at the surface.

As the magma nears the vent, it is cooling rapidly. Escape of gases thickens the magma, causing it to flow less easily. Pressure from below builds up. Explosions may result, blowing magma out of the vent.

An eroded batholith—*The central portion of South Dakota's Black Hills has been sculptured in a huge mass of granite uncovered by erosion. At the edges are "stumps" of sedimentary rock that covered the granite.*

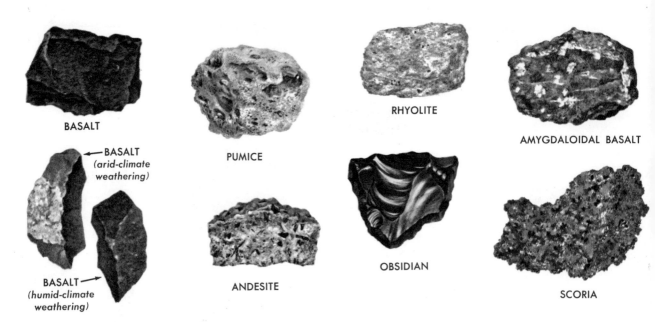

BASALT

BASALT
(arid-climate
weathering)

BASALT →
(humid-climate
weathering)

PUMICE

ANDESITE

RHYOLITE

OBSIDIAN

AMYGDALOIDAL BASALT

SCORIA

Rocks that Solidified Aboveground

As magma reaches the surface, it becomes what is called lava. Some is blown out of the vent and some flows out. Continued eruptions build up lava around the vent. If the vent is the opening of a pipelike passage, rather than a long fissure in the earth, the accumulating lava will build up gradually to become a cone-shaped hill—a volcanic cone. This has a crater, which is kept open by eruptions.

FORMS OF LAVA

Blown-out pieces of lava are called pyroclastics. Large roundish or pear-shaped blobs

are volcanic bombs. Large lava chunks with sizable holes left by escaping gases are scoria; smaller pieces are cinders. Frothy masses, very light in weight, are pumice. Small, hard lava stones are lapilli. Smaller pyroclastic bits are termed volcanic ash, and the very smallest are volcanic dust. Also among pyroclastics are volcanic blocks—fragments torn loose from the volcano's pipe. Pyroclastics may accumulate around a volcano as layers of ash and dust, with mixings of scoria, bombs, blocks, and lapilli.

Lava that flows over the edge of the crater runs down the sides of the cone. As this lava cools it solidifies into relatively strong rock—which is porous if the lava is gassy. Basaltic lava, the dark-colored type, flows easily and thus may spread widely over the countryside.

Basalt often cools as smooth-surfaced, ropy or pillowlike masses. Common in Hawaii and Iceland, it is known by the Hawaiian name *pahoehoe* (puh-HOY-hoy). The Hawaiian word *aa* (AH-ah) is applied to basalt lava with a very rough, clinkery surface.

As lava flows away from the vent, its surface hardens to a crust. For a time liquid lava may continue to flow beneath this crust, oozing out here and there through breaks. After all the

Lava "coils"—These examples of pahoehoe lava are among many to be seen at Craters of the Moon.

The sacred mountain—*Fujiyama, on Honshu, Japan, is a volcanic cone. It last erupted in 1707.*

lava has solidified, hollow passages called lava tubes may remain under the crust. Openings in the crust through which the lava flowed out remain as lava caves. In tubes and caves there may be lava "stalactites" hanging from the ceilings and lava "stalagmites" rising from the floor.

The pressure of hot, free-flowing lava may force up cooling, sluggish lava into bulges known as pressure ridges. Lava may be squeezed up through breaks in the crust as squeeze-ups. As dense basalt lava cools and contracts, it may break into long vertical columns with five or six (sometimes less) flat sides.

As already mentioned, basalt lava is rich in the dark, iron-bearing magnesian silicates, without quartz. Lava rock rich in quartz and feldspar is related to granite; a common form is rhyolite, a pink to grayish fine-grained rock. Granitic lava is thick, slow-moving, relatively quick to cool. It is often gassy, cooling as the very light porous rock pumice. A black variety is obsidian, formed when the lava cools so fast that it does not crystallize. A lava intermediate in chemical composition between basalt and granite forms the grayish rock andesite.

THE VOLCANIC CLOUD

A volcano in eruption usually produces a great windy cloud—mostly condensed moisture. Mixed with it are carbon dioxide and perhaps hydrogen and nitrogen, hydrochloric acid gas, and yellow sulfur vapor.

Quick flames—bluish, greenish, or yellowish—may light the cloud as hydrogen combines with oxygen in the air to form water, and as the heat makes the sulfur and other materials burn. Tons of hydrochloric acid, formed from hydrogen and chlorine, may be swept over the countryside by gusts of wind. Carbon dioxide may flow down the mountain and into villages, suffocating people as it did in Pompeii, Italy, during the great eruption of A.D. 79. With it go clouds of irritating sulfur dioxide.

At intervals lightning flashes through the cloud. The electricity is produced as bits of lava dust, violently blown around in the cloud,

Cinder cones and lava flows—*Such scenes are familiar in the Andes Mountains of South America. Some of the highest peaks are volcanoes recently active.*

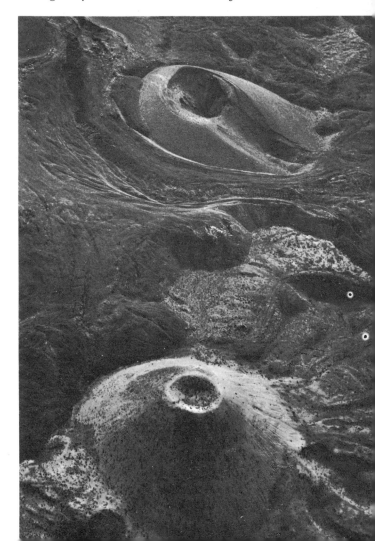

A "witch's caldron"—*The night-time activities of Mexico's Paricutín Volcano were a treat for sightseers, especially those who came with color film.*

A natural heating system—*This plant was built in New Zealand's Wairakei Valley to take advantage of abundant volcanic steam from underground.*

strike against one another, and also as steam condenses into water droplets and as chemicals react with one another.

Volcanic clouds always contain much moisture. Water from condensing steam may rush down the mountainside in torrents, picking up lava dust to form muddy floods.

CINDER CONES AND STRATO-VOLCANOES

Volcanoes that produce gassy, viscous, slow-flowing lava—the kind that makes rhyolite or andesite—have steep-sided cones. The reason is that such volcanoes tend to be explosive, producing lots of pyroclastics. Dust can be blown away, but the larger-caliber pyroclastics fall back into the crater or near it, thus building the steep-sided cone.

A volcanic hill made of pyroclastics is called a cinder cone or scoria cone. A good example is Capulin Mountain in New Mexico. Many young volcanoes are of this type. As a volcano gets older, lava flows may occur more often. These alternate with explosive eruptions, so that the hill or mountain is built up of alternating layers of flow lava and pyroclastics. Such volcanoes are called composite, or strato-, volcanoes. Most of them are located on continents near the ocean.

The Americas have many strato-volcanoes. One is Mt. Lassen, in northern California, the only volcano in the United States considered active. It began erupting in 1914 and continued active until 1921. It has since been quiet.

Chile, in South America, has Cotopaxi. This is the world's highest volcano—19,600 feet.

Mexico has dozens of volcanoes. One has the name visitors like to pronounce: Popocatepetl (poh-**POH**-kuh-**TAY**-puh-tl). More famous is Paricutín—a cinder cone studied by scientists practically from its birth.

THE SMOKING FIELD

Paricutín was born in 1943 in a mountainous region about 200 miles from Mexico City. Early in February a series of earthquakes began here, and each day they grew more violent. On February 20 a small column of "smoke" began rising from a farmer's field. As frightened villagers watched, the column grew. By the next day it had become a large cloud, pouring out of a cinder cone already 100 feet high. The cone grew as explosions every few seconds blew out rocks and dust.

During the next few days scientists arrived with notebooks, cameras, seismographs, and other equipment. As they looked on, the earth around the cone cracked and lava flows began. In time some flows spread six miles.

Showers of bombs and scoria built the cone to 500 feet in two weeks, 1,100 feet in three months, and 1,400 feet in the first year. On one day in 1945 the volcano belched out an estimated 16,000 tons of steam and 100,000 tons of lava.

All fields and woods for miles around were destroyed. Several villages were buried, including the town of Paricutín itself. Fortunately the inhabitants had enough warning to escape.

A.D. 79

The story was different for the people who were living near Mt. Vesuvius, Italy, in the year A.D. 79. In those days people did not recognize certain fateful warnings.

The mountain stands southeast of the blue bay of Naples. Two thousand years ago it was not known as a volcano. Farmers had planted vineyards and olive groves in the dark, fertile soils around the mountain and on its slopes. The mountain was green almost to the top. Vines and flowers grew even in the broad, circular hollow in the summit.

About A.D. 25 a Greek geographer and traveler, Strabo, visited this region. While walking high on the mountain he noticed patches of cinder-like material and "scorched" rocks. After making a few scholarly notes he went his way. Whether he talked to any of the farmers about the mountain no one knows.

In the year A.D. 63 the region was shaken by a series of earthquakes. Several towns suffered much property damage. Hardest hit was the small city of Pompeii, near the foot of the mountain. This town of 20,000 was a resort of wealthy Romans, who came here to relax in their villas overlooking the sea. The city's

Temple of Isis and other public buildings were shaken to pieces.

But where the soil is fertile and life is easy, people remain. Through sixteen years of occasional earthquakes people stayed on or near the mountain. Who would have dreamed that the cinderlike materials on the quiet slopes were a warning?

In August of A.D. 79 the quakes got worse. On the 24th, the quiet old mountain blew.

A lava cave—Here, at Valley of Fires, New Mexico, freely running lava poured from the side of a hardening flow, leaving a cave.

Awake again—In 1944 Mt. Vesuvius burst forth in its most violent eruption in 72 years. It produces a gassy, viscous, slow-flowing lava—the kind associated with violent, destructive eruptions.

The south side of the summit—that place of vines and flowers—vanished. Gas and dust poured out in enormous black clouds that darkened the sky for miles around. Down upon Pompeii swept gusts of poisonous gases, with showers of hot dust, rain, and mud. Terrified people fleeing through the streets were suffocated by the hundreds. Many were entombed in their homes as swirling pumice, like a devil's blizzard, piled up to depths of fifteen and twenty feet.

The town of Herculaneum, near Pompeii, fared no better. Steam from the volcanic cloud condensed into heavy rains, which rushed down the slopes, mixed with thousands of tons of dust, and poured through the streets. The floods

of hot mud did not stop until they had covered rooftops fifty to sixty-five feet high.

The mountain quieted, and the poisonous clouds blew away. All that remained was a smoking sea of mud and lava around the mountain's base, with a few blackened rooftops, and the mountain's plume of gases waving above all. In Pompeii alone no less than 2,000 people were entombed.

MILES

A shield volcano—*Mauna Loa is an enormous heap of flow lavas on the Pacific Ocean floor. The lavas, being very fluid, spread widely. Crater is higher above ocean floor than Mt. Everest is above sea level.*

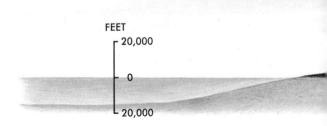

FEET
- 20,000
- 0
- 20,000

40

"SLEEPING FIRES"

In every volcano's career there comes a time when the upward flow of magma stops. Magma in the pipe cools and hardens, forming a plug. The volcano becomes dormant.

But a dormant volcano may be—as old Mt. Vesuvius was—treacherous. Suppose the underground pressure starts building up again, and rising magma is blocked by a hardened lava plug in the pipe. Earthquakes may again shake the region and the volcano may "blow."

Some of the most frightful disasters of history occurred when plugged volcanoes resumed business. That has happened several times with Vesuvius, and with Krakatoa and Pelée also.

The volcano of the island Krakatoa, in Indonesia, exploded in 1883. Steam, pumice, and ashes were shot 20 to 30 miles high. Ships in Sunda Strait were showered with phosphorescent mud. A large part of the island was destroyed, and earthquakes started a great sea wave that drowned 30,000 people on Java and Sumatra. About 4½ cubic miles of pumice was blown out—enough to make a stone block four miles long, a mile wide, and more than a mile high. Dust blown into the stratosphere was carried by winds entirely around the world, and for many months it caused sunrises and sunsets of unusual redness.

Mt. Pelée, on the island of Martinique in the West Indies, erupted in 1902 after fifty years of calm. Very stiff lava was pushed out of the top as a "spine," or tower, 1,000 feet high. Its enormous weight, added to the gas pressure beneath, broke off the side of the cone. Out of the hole shot a gigantic red-hot cloud of ash, sand, and steam. Flashing with lightning, it swept down over the countryside at 60 miles per hour. The town of St. Pierre, capital of Martinique, was engulfed, and all the 28,000 inhabitants except one—a man in the underground jail—were suffocated or burned to death. In the harbor, the water boiled and ships were overturned.

Perhaps the greatest eruption in human history was the one that occurred on the island of Thera, in the Mediterranean Sea, about 1470 B.C. It demolished half of the 40,000-acre island and started a sea wave which, according to archeologists, laid waste the island of Crete, 62 miles away, destroying the Minoan civilization. The explosion has been estimated as four times as powerful as the Krakatoa event.

SHIELD VOLCANOES

Volcanoes that produce mostly basaltic, free-flowing lava tend to be of the "shield" type. Most of these volcanoes rise from ocean bottoms. The perfect model is Hawaii's Mauna Loa, the largest volcano in the world.

The Hawaiian Islands are all of volcanic origin. Here, during the past two million years, hot basalt has poured from cracks in the Pacific Ocean floor. The lava has piled up flow upon flow. The tops of lava piles (some now capped with coral) are the Hawaiian Islands of today.

Mauna Loa has grown up where a number of big cracks in the Pacific crustal plate intersect. The volcano has taken perhaps a million years to grow to its present height—much longer than the average cone volcano. The very fluid lava has spread far before hardening, so that the mountain has not developed steep sides. It is a relatively low, rounded mound—a shield.

that feeds the main crater. Eruptions in 1959 to 1960 produced fountains of lava 1,900 feet high, filling an old crater to a depth of 365 feet. Four years later the crust on the lava lake was 50 feet thick, and the temperature beneath it about 2,000 degrees Fahrenheit.

On Kilauea's summit, in Hawaii Volcanoes National Park, is the Hawaiian Volcanoes Observatory. Here geologists study all aspects of volcanic activity. Seismographs record earth tremors; tiltmeters measure changes in the slope of the ground; pyrometers measure temperatures below ground and in lava flows. With other instruments geologists analyze the chemical compositions of erupted materials.

IS THERE ANY WARNING?

Scientists have been studying volcanoes for over a hundred years. Observatories such as those on Kilauea, Vesuvius, and Mt. Pelée have revealed many secrets of volcanic activity. Although eruptions have no schedule, the volcano experts have sometimes been able to predict eruptions and thus save lives and property.

A fairly sure sign of trouble is a series of earthquakes near a volcano. These, with tilting of the ground, indicate that sections of the

The bottom of this enormous heap of basalt is 70 miles in diameter. The crater, 13,680 feet above the sea, is two miles long and a mile wide. Since the sea here is about 17,000 feet deep, the mountain rises nearly 30,000 feet in all—almost six miles—above the ocean floor.

The great crater of Mauna Loa has recently been quiet. But on the mountain's east side, at an elevation of 4,000 feet, is the active crater Kilauea. It has a pipe separate from the one

How a Volcanic Neck is Made

Magma solidifies in cone as volcano becomes inactive

Solidified "neck" is exposed as erosion removes soft cone material

Neck stands above landscape long after cone is gone

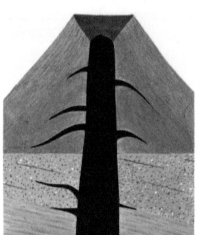

"Fossil volcano"—New Mexico's Ship Rock, 1,640 feet high, is a famous volcanic neck—the remains of a mass of magma that solidified in the throat of a dying volcano. The Southwest features many "necks."

crust are being disturbed by deep forces. New channels may be opening up for magma. Wells in the area may go dry—indicating new cracks underground, allowing ground water to descend deeper. Water reaching hot rock may turn to steam and boost the pressure, causing quakes.

Lava coming from a volcano at a time of mild activity can be analyzed for hints as to what is going on below. An eruption may be hinted also by changes in ground magnetism in the vicinity of the volcano.

WHEN VOLCANOES DIE

A volcano may become active as Vesuvius did even after centuries of calm. It may be active for a number of years and then, like Paricutín, quiet down. Or it may perform practically without a halt century after century. The volcano on Stromboli Island, north of Sicily, has been popping mildly since the days of ancient Rome. Its friendly glow has earned it the name "Lighthouse of the Mediterranean."

As volcanoes become extinct and erosion takes over, the cone is worn lower. In time it may be completely eroded away.

A familiar relic of extinct volcanoes is the volcanic neck. This is a hard mass of lava that cooled in the volcano's pipe when it ceased activity. The hard mass remains after the softer parts of the cone have eroded away.

One of the San Francisco Peaks in Arizona, north of Flagstaff, is a volcanic neck. Better known is Ship Rock, in northwestern New Mexico—1,640 feet high. Running out from this volcanic neck, like spokes of a big wheel, are three long arms of rock—dikes. These are of magma that "froze" in fissures below the cone and has since been uncovered by erosion.

Volcanic necks that rise high and steep above surrounding land have been in past times favorite sites for fortifications and churches. Edinburgh Castle in Scotland is built on a neck called Castle Rock. The little chapel of St. Michel in Auvergne province in France is another building on a neck.

The best-known volcanic relic in the United States probably is Crater Lake, in Oregon. It lies in a great hole in the top of Mt. Mazama, an extinct volcano of the Cascade Range. Some 6,500 years ago Mt. Mazama, then about 12,000 feet high, blew some 10 cubic miles of pumice into the sky. The crater walls, undermined by removal of lava, collapsed, so that the original crater was much enlarged.

A crater enlarged in this way is known as a caldera (kawl-DER-uh). Mt. Mazama's caldera is 6 miles wide and 4,000 feet deep. From the beautiful blue lake rises a cinder cone, Wizard Island, produced by eruptions after the caldera was developed.

Even larger is Valles Caldera in the volcanic Jemez Mountains of New Mexico. It is more than twice as wide as the Mazama caldera but is less scenic.

Numerous extinct cinder cones are seen today in the West. At Craters of the Moon, Idaho,

A volcano that became a lake—*Collapse of the crater walls of Mt. Mazama, about 6,500 years ago, left the caldera now occupied by Crater Lake, 2,000 feet deep. Wizard Island (right center) is a cinder cone formed later. Inset shows profile of mountain as it may have been before crater walls collapsed.*

Fumarole cores—*The Pinnacles, near Mt. Mazama, consist of volcanic materials that hardened within fumaroles. The pinnacles took form as softer surrounding materials eroded away.*

there are cones as much as 600 feet high. Cones are to be seen also in regions flanking the Rocky Mountains, in western Texas, and in the states farther west.

FISSURE FLOWS

Basaltic lava erupted from long fissures, rather than volcanic pipes, may not form volcanic cones. It may simply flow out over the land in wide, bubbling sheets or streams. Much igneous activity has been of this sort.

Fissure flows may be as disastrous as eruptions from big volcanoes. Iceland, for example, once suffered frightful damage and loss of life from such a flow. Iceland lies astride the Mid-atlantic Ridge, a submarine volcanic range split by a long fissure. In Iceland, in 1783, fast-moving basaltic lava poured out of this fissure along a stretch of 20 miles and spread to distances as great as 40 miles on each side. A fifth of Iceland's population was wiped out.

THE LAVA SEAS

The fissure flow in Iceland was nothing compared to some flows that occurred before the age of man. In the Northwest is the Columbia Plateau, a highland of basalt covering areas of five states—Washington, Oregon, Idaho, Nevada, California. Layered lavas cover about 200,000 square miles, more than four times the area of New York State. The amount of lava poured out is estimated at about 100,000 cubic miles. Valleys nearly a mile deep were filled. Since the period of activity, some 20 million years ago, the Snake and Columbia rivers have cut as much as 4,000 feet down into the plateau.

The remains of a mass of basalt covering 600,000 square miles make a broad, curving path reaching from Greenland through Iceland, to the Inner Hebrides near Scotland, and down to Antrim in Northern Ireland. These flows, which are as much as 1,500 feet thick, lie mostly under the ocean.

45

holes called fumaroles (from Spanish, "to smoke"). As the gases emerge and cool on the surface, they deposit minerals which they had dissolved underground—sulfur, copper, lead, even iron.

Famous among fumarole regions is the Valley of Ten Thousand Smokes in Alaska. Mt. Etna in Italy is noted for the 200 fumaroles on its smoking slopes.

Death Valley, California, has a few fumaroles. Carbon dioxide produced by them settles in low areas and can be a danger for travelers.

Among the thickest lava beds ever discovered are those in the Lake Superior area. The basalt is in places 50,000 feet—nearly 10 miles —deep. Part of this frozen lava sea forms the Keweenawaw Peninsula, famous for copper.

FUMAROLES: THE "SMOKERS"

In active volcanic areas, gases from magma may emerge at the surface through fissures or

HOT SPRINGS AND GEYSERS

Water that passes over hot rock underground and emerges at the surface makes a hot spring. Usually the water is rainwater that has worked down into the ground through cracks. Because of heat and pressure, the water dissolves more minerals than it would normally. These minerals may give the springs medicinal value, and so the region may become a health resort. Hot

Remnants of a "lava sea"—*In the gorge of the Columbia River, in Washington, are exposed the edges of some of the lava layers that make up the Columbia Plateau.*

Old Faithful—*Yellowstone's famous geyser was named for its custom of performing at approximately hourly intervals, decade after decade.*

Springs, Arkansas, is one such resort. Japan and New Zealand have many hot-spring resorts.

A familiar and beautiful sight in some old volcanic regions is the geyser. Every American has heard of Yellowstone National Park's Old Faithful, which spouts some 15,000 gallons of steam and water 150 feet into the air at intervals of 61 to 67 minutes.

Beneath every geyser is a looping channel, running down into a zone of hot rock. Ground water percolates down into this channel and is heated. For a while the weight of the water in the channel keeps the heated water in the bottom from changing to steam. Finally, however, some water gets so hot that it does change to steam. The change is sudden, and because the steam takes up much more space than the water, there is an explosion in the channel.

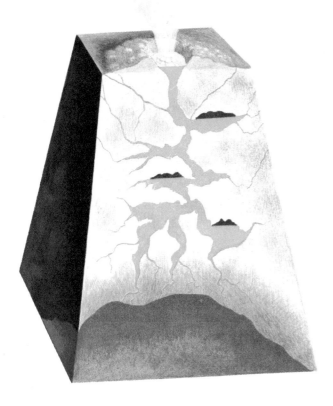

Anatomy of a geyser—*Underground channels fill with ground water. When this is turned to steam by volcanic heat, an eruption occurs.*

This ejects water at the surface. Now there is more room for steam to form below, more water changes to steam, and still more water is ejected at the surface. The process continues until most of the water in the channel has been ejected. Then the eruption ceases, only to be resumed when the channel has refilled.

Hot springs and geysers are features of what are called "dying" volcanic areas. Here magma is no longer rising to the surface, but there is enough heat underground to boil water. Typical of such areas is Yellowstone National Park, where volcanoes were active until a few million years ago. Similar areas are found in New Zealand. Iceland, very rich in hot springs and geysers, is a volcanic area which is partly "dying" and partly active.

47

The Shaping of the Land

RUGGED mountains, deep canyons, huge valleys—these seem to suggest an ancient time when earthquakes broke and rumpled the land. No wonder people believed for so long that our planet was shaped by cataclysms. We know now that most landscapes have been shaped slowly by forces that are at work still. The action of air and water wears down highlands, and gravity moves the debris down to lower places and deposits it there. Erosion and deposition, mainly, account for landscapes as different as the Badlands of South Dakota, the Great Plains, the carved seacoasts of Maine and Oregon, and the rolling countryside of Ohio.

A WORLD OF CHANGE

Until less than two centuries ago, even scholars who were thinking scientifically believed that Earth was created in a series of cataclysms and has remained about the same ever since. Such a belief should not really surprise us. Landscapes are unlikely to change much during the lifetime of an individual. Outlines of mountains, large valleys, and seacoasts are much the same now as in the time of our grandfathers—or Julius Caesar—or even early man. Landshaping processes are mostly so slow that we hardly notice them.

The power of running water to erode the land was noticed by Aristotle and other ancient thinkers. But the first observer to appreciate the great works of erosion was the Scottish physician and farmer, James Hutton. With a scientist's curiosity he investigated the soils and rocks around him. He compared rock strata and fossils, observed the sea's destructive work on shores, and watched streams cutting into the land and spreading flood debris. To him, Earth's surface showed the results of long, long erosion and deposition.

Hutton published in 1795 one of the great early books on geology: *Theory of the Earth*. He pictured Earth as possibly hundreds of thousands of years old—old enough for the forces of erosion to wear away mountains and carry their remains into the sea, from which new mountains could arise. Earth-shaping forces are still at work. And men, like living things of the past, will become fossils for future ages.

It was an awesome picture—this Earth so old, Hutton said, that it seemed to have "no beginning, no prospect of an end." Such an idea seemed against human experience. A generation after Hutton, Sir Charles Lyell was still trying to convince other scientists of the powers of erosion.

Today, with two centuries of geological science behind us, it is still not easy to think of hills, valleys, and plains as the erosional ruin of former worlds. But we can make a beginning.

WEARING DOWN A HILL

Could a granite hill rust? Could it crumble away like an old tin can outdoors?

Water, with oxygen from the air, will rust the can. Water and air likewise will keep eating away at a granite hill, softening it and crumbling it, grain by grain. A granite hill does not "rust," but over millions of years it will crumble away.

"City of spires"—Bryce Canyon, in southern Utah, testifies to the power of running water in the shaping of land. The climate is dry; but when rain does come, gullying is rapid because the rock is soft and vegetation sparse. This view is from Inspiration Point. In the background, left, is Table Cliffs Plateau.

49

Weathering and erosion of granite—*The Needles, in South Dakota's Black Hills, show the influence of many vertical joints (fractures) in the rock.*

Our granite hill—any hill—is under attack by many agents. Rainwater flows over bedrock and dissolves a slight amount of it. Also, the water contains oxygen and carbon dioxide from air and therefore can attack rock chemically. Tree roots work into cracks and widen them, just as tree roots can raise a sidewalk. Animals may burrow into the hill. Body wastes from animals corrode rock a little, and so do decaying remains of plants and animals.

Granite is a rock that forms very deep in the crust and under enormous pressure. As the granite is uncovered by erosion, the removal of weight reduces pressure on it. The inside of the granite mass expands, causing shell-like slabs to break off the surface. This is a kind of weathering called exfoliation.

Rock exposed to hot sun for many hours heats up. If the surface is rapidly cooled—by rain, for example—the rock near the surface shrinks faster than the rock deeper inside. Grains or flakes of rock break off.

Weathering and erosion of granite—*At Sylvan Lake, near The Needles (above), the joints are more widely spaced, and more horizontal than vertical. Hence the granite is shaped into broad, rounded forms.*

"Frost flowers"—*Water from melted snow freezes in the ground, expanding and forming crystals that push up the soil and pry apart rocks.*

Exfoliation of granite—*Slabs break off as the bedrock, uncovered by erosion, expands. Freezing and chemical action break off flakes and grains.*

When water freezes it expands, so that the ice takes up about one ninth more space than the water did. The force of this expansion is tremendous—it can split boulders weighing tons. So when water freezes in cracks in rock, it makes them wider and breaks loose big chunks of the rock.

Rain falls on the hill. Fallen drops run together to make thousands of little rills. These pick up tiny bits of stone and carry them along. Water in gullies becomes streams strong enough to move sand and pebbles. This material scrapes the bedrock, breaking off more small bits. And so the destruction goes on, as rills run into gullies to make brooks, and as brooks run down into valleys to form rivers.

WATER WORKING EVERYWHERE

It takes millions of years to erode away a large granite hill. But where rock is softer, erosion is faster.

Everyone has seen what a heavy rain can do to a clay bank along a highway. Farmers dread heavy rains that cut gullies into sloping fields. In our backyards we have seen little canyons cut by rushing rainwater streams.

The regions called badlands show amazing work by water. In North America these grim yet beautiful landscapes are found especially in the Dakotas, Nebraska and Wyoming, and Alberta. They suggest that giant claws

"Honeycombed" rock—*Percolation of water through this soluble limestone made countless cavities.*

raked through Earth's crust, cutting ragged ridges and steep-walled valleys.

Badlands develop in regions of relatively light rainfall and weak bedrock, usually shale or sandstone. There is little vegetation except scattered small plants. When rain does fall, little of it can sink into the dusty ground. Most of the water mixes with dust and rushes downslope in sheets or streams. Gullies are cut relatively fast in the soft rock, and loose material piles up at the foot of gullies. A single hard rain in badlands may do more erosion than the rains of many years on forested hills.

Flat as a table: a mesa—*This mesa near Springdale, Utah, is typical of many in this region of horizontal rock layers. Note the vertical cliff along the edges of the strong layer that caps the mesa. Long erosion of the mesa will convert it into a butte.*

GOBLINS, MESAS, AND BUTTES

In dry regions, especially, we often see bedrock eroded into forms suggesting goblins, animals, faces, and other things. Usually these forms develop on rock that consists of layers of varying resistance to erosion. Rainwater running down in vertical fractures widens them and carves the rock into blocks and pillars. Weathering and rainwash on the sides of the blocks and pillars wear the edges of the layers unevenly because of differences in resistance, and thus the odd profiles are created. These landforms may become smoothed at the bottom by blowing sand.

Deep erosion in horizontal rock layers may produce wide, flat-topped highlands called mesas. Usually a mesa (Spanish MAY-suh, "table") is capped by a layer of strong rock lying on weaker rock. Often the stronger layer is of hardened lava. Relatively rapid erosion of the edges of weaker layers keeps the sides of the mesa steep.

In some bedrocks vertical fractures are close together. Erosion in these fractures gradually carves the rock mass into hills that are steep-sided and cover a small area compared to their height. Such hills are called buttes. Some of them are the last remains of long-eroded mesas.

These landforms are typical of the Colorado Plateau, particularly in Colorado, Utah, and Arizona. Similar landforms have been carved from horizontal strata in more humid areas, as in the Catskills in New York state and along major rivers in Illinois and Ohio. However, in humid areas landform profiles tend to be smoothed by vegetation.

GRAVITY: THE LEVELER

Every particle of stone on a slope is being pulled by gravity. A short rainstorm can move countless particles an inch—others maybe a hundred feet—downslope. A small snowslide in winter provides another downward ride. The blowing force of wind, the scampering and burrowing of animals, the wedging force of ice, the swelling and shrinking of rock as temperatures change, the swelling and shrinking of soil as it freezes and thaws—such events tend to keep rock material moving downslope year after year.

At the base of a cliff we usually find a heap of broken rock. This was broken loose from the cliff by weathering, and fell. It is called talus.

Sandstone "goblins"—*Figures shaped by rainwash in Devil's Garden, near Escalante, Utah, suggest goblins talking. Note human figure (in white shirt).*

Sculptures in clay—*Bleak but beautiful are the landscapes called "badlands." These are commonly cut by rainwater torrents in slopes of soft rock. This view is in Badlands National Monument, South Dakota.*

Lava pinnacles—*Weathering and rainwash shaped these rhyolite masses at Chiricahua National Monument, Arizona. Human figure (center) gives scale.*

It is temporarily at rest; some day gravity will find a way to move it lower.

In some places gravity works with shocking swiftness. Take, for example, a hillside with a thick layer of clay lying on sloping bedrock. Clay gets slippery when wet. After rains the clay may start to slip on the bedrock. Faster it moves, and faster—and we have a slide, piling up a mass of clay below.

Rivers touch off landslides by undermining cliffs. Earthquakes start slides by shaking the ground. Frost-wedging and the melting of heavy snows are other causes.

Man starts slides by blasting in mines, quarries, and roadcuts. Small slides or flows of surface material become likely where a slope has been cleared of trees and brush, because their roots help to hold water and keep soil in place.

Some highlands are formed of folded layers of bedrock, tilted steeply and cracked. If water works in between the layers, they may begin to slip. This is what happened years ago in the Gros Ventre range, near the little town of Kelly, Wyoming.

The Gros Ventres are low, rounded mountains topped with soft red sandstone and shale. During 1925 there were heavy rains. In June a great mass of the red rock slid down into the valley of the Gros Ventre River. This stream, partly blocked by earlier slides, had formed

Some Features Created by Weathering and Erosion

Hogback: Erosion of soft rock exposes hard stratum as ridge.

Dome: Flakes and slabs break off granite.

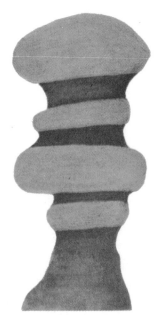

Goblin: Soft layers are worn away faster than hard ones.

Mesa: Hard cap rock protects softer rock beneath.

Needles: Weathering in close vertical fractures.

Nature's fancy—*Delicate Arch, at Arches National Monument, Utah, was made by the tunneling action of running water and wind, along with weathering.*

Slide Lake. For two years this lake kept rising behind the higher dam formed by the new slide. By May 1927 it was three miles long.

Then, suddenly, this dam gave way, and a tremendous torrent rushed down through the valley and swept over Kelly. Houses were washed away and several people were drowned, as well as many livestock. Today Slide Lake is smaller and all is peaceful, but on the mountain slope above the lake is a great red scar.

TURTLE MOUNTAIN

The worst of all North American landslides was the slide of 1903 at Frank, a little coal-mining town in Alberta, Canada.

Creeping vs. falling—*On a gentle slope (left) rocks creep down by slight movements over centuries. On a steep slope (right) they fall or tumble down, making talus. This mountain road is near Llanberis, Wales.*

Mass wasting in earnest—*The Tunnel Road Landslide of 1950, on California State Highway 24, resulted from the soaking of masses of clay and gravel by rains. Such slides are common in this vicinity.*

55

Above Frank looms Turtle Mountain. Its upper part is formed of limestone strata that slant down steeply toward the town. The layers are much cracked, and the spaces between them have been widened by ice wedging and by the dissolving action of underground water.

Early one morning in 1903, men were blasting in the mine near the mountain's base. All at once there was a trembling of the earth— not from the blasting. High on the steep slope a block of limestone a half mile square and several hundred feet thick was slipping. Before the townspeople knew what was happening, the gigantic stone block plunged downward. It hit the valley bottom and shattered. Like a breaking wave the jumble of rocks roared over part of the town and crashed against the opposite side of the valley a full two miles away.

In less than two minutes it was all over. There were 70 dead and missing in Frank. The miners underground were all unhurt.

In the Alps mountain slopes are steep, rock layers often tilted vertical or nearly so. Landslides are common and so are snow avalanches. In spring, ice and rock under thick layers of melting snow become slippery. Even a breeze or a climber's shout, it is said, may jar the snow layers enough to start an avalanche.

For people in some Alpine villages the experience of digging out home, family, and friends—alive or dead—is all too familiar.

GONE WITH THE WIND

Strong winds can roll boulders and push pebbles. They lift some sand grains to heights of six or seven feet and make others skip along the ground. Dust can be lifted miles high and carried across oceans.

Farmers in the midwestern United States have seen sad proof of the power of moving air. In periods of drought, winds sweeping across dusty

Nature's dumps—*Scenic rock heaps at Bow Lake, Banff National Park, Canada, are "talus cones." They consist of rock fragments broken off by the action of water freezing in crevices in the cliffs.*

fields have stolen thousands of tons of valuable soil. In March 1936 skies over New York City were half-darkened by soil blowing in from the so-called Dust Bowl of the south-central states, 1,300 miles away. In a few years the land level in some Dust Bowl areas was lowered by as much as 3 to 4 feet.

When Cape Cod was settled in the seventeenth century, it was heavily forested, with rich virgin soil. As farmers cleared the land, the winds blew away more and more topsoil, and by the mid-1800s most of it was gone. The winds kept blowing, and the Cape's harbors—vital to fishermen and whalers—were filling up. Only strenuous efforts by Cape Codders, in-cluding widespread planting of tough beach grass and young trees, saved their homeland from becoming a desert.

The power of wind to lower land is greatest in deserts, where vegetation is sparse. In places like the Mohave Desert and Death Valley wind has blown away so much soil that plants are left standing on their roots like stilts. In southern Wyoming some areas are said to have been lowered 150 feet by wind in the past century. Parts of the Libyan Desert in Africa have been lowered 420 feet below the level of the Mediterranean Sea.

Wind carrying sand acts like a sandblasting machine. Sharp sand particles driven against

Dammed by a mudflow—*A mass of rain-soaked volcanic ash in the San Juan Mountains, Colorado, flowed five miles down valley, blocked the canyon of the Gunnison River, and formed Lake San Cristobal. The mudflow was dubbed "Slumgullion."*

rock surfaces gradually wear these down. Shallow caves are cut in cliffs, and the lower parts of rock pillars and arches are smoothed. Broad, level areas of bedrock in deserts also become smoothed.

Natural sandblasting cannot carve out large pillars, arches, "fins," and other such desert forms from larger rock masses. These features are first cut out by weathering and running water, then more finely sculptured by blowing sand near their bases.

WIND AS A BUILDER

In deserts and along open beaches the wind is a builder. Given plenty of loose sand, it piles this up into dunes, tears down the dunes, then builds them up again.

Shapes of dunes depend on wind direction, wind strength, and the kind of material being blown. The common barchan, or crescent dune, has a gentle slope on the windward side. As the wind goes up this slope it loses speed and its ability to move the sand. The sand drops and slides down the lee side of the dune, building a steep slope there.

Once a dune is started, it can grow very large, if sand in the area is plentiful. Then, perhaps, one strong wind may blow it away.

Dunes can be compared to snowdrifts, but may build much higher. American dunes rise to heights of 300 feet—for example, at Great Sand Dunes National Monument, in southern Colorado. The Sahara has dunes 600 to 700 feet high.

In any region, the wind blows more from one direction than from others. Thus in time most of the sand in a desert may be blown to one side. The sands of Great Sand Dunes National Monument have been blown from the west side of the San Luis Valley to the foot of the Sangre de Cristo Mountains on the east side. There they are trapped and accumulate to greater and greater depths.

Traveling dunes become a menace. Many a cottage along a seashore has been buried by a marching dune. The same has happened to farms and ranches in drought-ridden areas. Along sandy seashores, such as those of Oregon and North Carolina, marching dunes are burying hundreds of square miles of forest.

Once a farm—*This homestead in the Dust Bowl, in Morton County, Kansas, was one of thousands ruined by drought and wind in the 1930's. Some Dust Bowl soil was blown all the way to the Atlantic. Since then, many farms have been restored by means of irrigation.*

The making of barchans—*Arrows indicate how air currents transporting sand make dunes.*

LOESS DEPOSITS

In areas toward which prevailing winds blow, deposits of loess may be found. This tan or buff earth consists of very fine rock particles—silt. Much of it probably was produced by the scraping action of glaciers on rock. Winds carried the loess from highlands and dropped it on lower areas.

Thick loess deposits are likely to be hard-packed, with vertical joints like those in some bedrocks. Joints divide the loess into smooth-sided vertical columns. In sides of roadcuts columns may stand firmly, almost like masonry.

Loess deposits up to 40 feet thick are found in the Mississippi Valley. But the world's greatest deposits are in China, where they reach depths of several hundred feet. Probably this loess came from the Gobi Desert.

A world of sand—*At Great Sand Dunes National Monument, in southern Colorado, prevailing winds from the west have piled sand into huge dunes at the foot of the Sangre de Cristo Mountains.*

Endlessly gnawing away at the land's edges is the sea. Waves, currents, and the dissolving power of water are the sea's teeth. Only repeated land uplifts, through the ages, have prevented the ocean from eroding the continents down to sea level.

Ordinary ocean waves are produced by wind. A wind blowing at 30 miles an hour across a wide area of ocean for one day can make waves 15 feet high and 300 feet long. Even after traveling 2,000 miles these waves will be 2½ feet high. Waves do travel thousands of miles, and so, even when there is no wind blowing against a coast, waves keep coming in.

At sea, water particles in a wave move in vertical, nearly circular paths parallel to the wind direction. The wave moves forward, but the particles do not. As the wave comes in to shallow water, the particles begin striking bottom, and the lower part of the wave is slowed. The upper part spills forward, forming a breaker.

As every surfer knows, a breaking ocean wave is powerful. Impacts of storm waves can break off chunks of rock from a sea cliff, and with-

drawing water can suck out more rock. Wave water wedges into crevices, making rock shatter. Rock fragments are tossed by waves and hurled against the cliff. Sand and gravel, moved by currents, scrape the cliff below the water level. Thus, by various processes, waves and currents dig out the base of a sea cliff, often making a notch in it. Overhangs of rock break off and fall. During centuries the cliff is gradually eroded back.

A cliff's retreat may leave a rock platform extending seaward from the cliff's base. This platform, known as a wave-cut bench or terrace, is usually at about the water level. When onshore winds are blowing, waves and currents drag rock waste back and forth over the bench, smoothing it and gradually lowering it. In time, land uplift may raise the bench above sea level, as has happened along the Oregon and California coasts.

A rock cliff may be eroded back only a foot or so per century. Sandy or clayey bluffs erode much more rapidly. The sandy east shore of Cape Cod is retreating about one foot per year. During the September 1944 hurricane, the

Erosion on seacoasts—*Along some seacoasts, waves and currents work mainly with sand, gravel, and cobbles, building beaches and bars. Such coasts often are areas recently risen above sea level. Along other coasts, especially where the land has been sinking, the sea is attacking rocky cliffs.*

ADVANCING SHORELINE

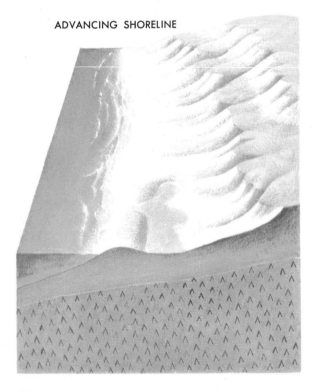

RETREATING SHORELINE

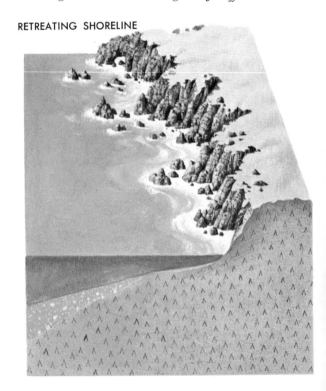

A sea sculpture—*Arch Rock, in Depoe Bay on the Oregon coast, is the remnant of an eroded headland.*

Cape's Nauset cliffs were cut back no less than 50 feet in some places.

Parts of a cliff where the rock is relatively weak are cut back faster. Deep, narrow inlets may be cut into cliffs along joints. Caves may form where the sea attacks pockets of weaker rock. As a breaker plunges into a cave, water may burst noisily from a blowhole—an opening in the cave's roof.

Zones of weaker rock become the locations of coves, bays, and bights. These tend to "trap" rock waste being moved along shore by waves and currents. Trapped rock waste accumulates to form a beach.

Coastal indentations are separated by headlands, or promontories. Eventually the sea breaks through a headland; thus tunnels and arches may form. When tops of arches collapse, the sides are left standing as "stacks."

Along rocky coasts the sea does its most beautiful sculpturing. In North America the best scenery of this kind is between Newfoundland and Maine, and from Alaska to California. Shores of the British Isles are mostly rocky and scenic, as are those of Norway. Southern France and other countries bordering the Mediterranean also have scenic coasts.

Saving a beach—*The sand and clay of Cape Cod, deposited by melting glacier ice during the recent ice age, are retreating before the attack of the Atlantic Ocean. Little can be done to slow the pace of destruction by waves and currents, but beach grass has been planted to slow the lowering of the land by wind. These rows of beach grass are on Nauset Beach.*

The work of currents—*Shoals near the west end of Nantucket are sandbars made by waves and currents.*

BEACHES

Erosion of sea cliffs produces quantities of rock waste—sand, gravel, cobbles, and larger fragments. Rivers emptying into the sea bring more sediments. Waves and currents along the shore work this material over and over, smoothing the rock fragments, making them smaller and smaller. This material makes beaches.

The underwater part of a beach is a wide terrace of loose rock waste which waves and currents drag back and forth. On the terrace parallel to the shore is a sand or gravel ridge called the longshore bar, made by breakers as they dig into the sand and pile it up. Above the

water line the beach slopes up to another terrace, the summer berm, formed by swash from ordinary waves. Farther back there is usually a higher berm—the winter berm—made by storm waves. Beyond that is a sea cliff, and still farther back, perhaps, a gravel beach ridge built up during the most violent storms.

Along a beach are many temporary features to notice. Swash marks are thin, low ridges of sand left at the highest reach of swash from waves. Ripple marks are wavy ridges of sand made by waves or currents. Rill marks are little channels cut by streams running down the beach at low tide or after a backwash phase. Beach cusps are series of low, rounded mounds, pointed at the waterline, made by wave and current action in the tidal zone.

Beaches themselves may be short-lived. Usually waves hit a beach at an angle, sweeping sand down the shore. Backwash makes longshore currents, often powerful enough to move huge quantities of sand. During a storm an exposed beach may lose much sand—only to get a new supply during the next storm.

In time, prevailing winds may move so much sand downshore that walls, docks, and even buildings near the shoreline are undermined and destroyed. To reduce sand loss, barrier walls called jetties or groins may be built seaward from the shore. Sea walls built parallel to the shoreline break the force of storm waves.

Where sand is plentiful, long sand ridges, called barriers, may be built by the sea's action parallel to the shore. Some grow to become long, relatively permanent barrier islands, as along the Atlantic Coast from New Jersey to Florida.

Deposition may build a curving sand ridge—a "spit"—from the tip of a headland. The spit may curve to form one or more hooks. Some spits grow across the mouth of a bay to create a baymouth bar.

Between a sand barrier and the mainland is a body of water called a lagoon. Currents of tide water bring in sediments through openings in the bar. Sediments are deposited in a quiet

Islands in sand—*At Seal Rocks State Park, Oregon, dikes are exposed as the sea erodes volcanic materials.*

A retreating coastline—*The coasts of Cornwall, England, have sunk in recent geologic time, and the sea is cutting into rock cliffs. This view, including many sea stacks, is at Lizard Point.*

lagoon to form a marsh with channels through which tide water moves in and out.

An island near the mainland may block sediment moving downshore. Thus may develop a tombolo—a sandbar connecting the island to the shore.

Through geologic time an irregular coastline tends to be straightened by erosion. Headlands are attacked especially hard by the sea because they are exposed. Coves and bays tend to be filled in with sediment. But at any time during the straightening process a rising or sinking of the coast may occur, producing a new shore that is irregular.

Two types of seashores—*Southern Connecticut has sunk relative to the ocean, which has invaded river valleys to make numerous estuaries. The coast is of the "ria" type. The shores are on bedrock. In contrast is the north shore of Long Island, which is on sand and clay. Here waves and currents have shaped the loose material to make bars, spits, and bays.*

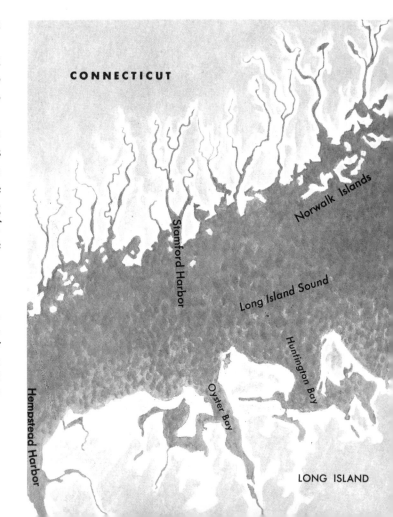

A water-carved underworld—*Fantastic stalactites and stalagmites in Luray Caverns, Virginia, testify to the dissolving power of ground water. Caverns are common in most regions where bedrock is limestone.*

Ground Water

MOST people have seen the drilling of a well. A pipe is driven into the ground and sooner or later, at a depth of 20 feet, or 50, or maybe 200, the drillers strike water. The pipe reaches a zone underground where the soil or rock is full of water, like a sponge.

A driller can strike water almost anywhere if he drills deep enough. Even beneath the Sahara there is some water. Our planet's crust is wet not only under the oceans but beneath all land surfaces.

The ancients thought most water in the crust must come from "reservoirs" underground where it was "made." Today we know relatively little water is created underground: such water is "juvenile," formed chemically from magma. Most water underground has worked down from the surface.

Aristotle, more than two thousand years ago, taught that water is "raised" by the Sun from the oceans, then falls as rain on mountains to feed rivers. Leonardo da Vinci was the first to understand that rainwater can seep underground and form streams and "reservoirs" there. Thus Aristotle and Leonardo together envisioned what we call the water cycle.

TRAVELS OF WATER

The snow and rain that fall each year would be enough to cover our globe with water 3½ feet deep. Deserts such as the Sahara and the Arabian Desert get only a few inches of water annually. Regions of average rainfall, such as the eastern United States, get about 40 inches. Parts of India and some other very humid areas get 30 to 40 feet.

Where water comes from—*A drawing in the 17th-century book* Cataractae Mundi *("Waterfalls of the World") attempts to explain the origin of water. Neptune, God of the Sea, pours water into a monster which then spouts it high over land and sea.*

Some rainwater collects in streams and lakes. Some trickles underground. Much is used by plants and animals. Surface water is soon evaporated into the air, and part of it falls again as rain or snow. Sooner or later, all water that falls as rain or snow gets back to the sea.

It may take a million years for one particular molecule of water to get from sea to land and back to the sea again. After falling from a cloud it may be in a river for a time, then underground, later in a lake or swamp, then up in the atmosphere, now in the body of an animal, and again in a river. Much of the time it may be in the crust as "ground water."

Water falling onto the ground percolates, or works down, between soil grains. If the grains are relatively large, as in sand, the water percolates relatively fast. If the grains are clay, downward movement is slower. Some water molecules

stick to the grains by electrical attraction: the smaller the grains, the stronger the attraction. Thus soil may remain damp for days after rain.

Descending water may come to bedrock. This may have many tiny connecting tunnels between grains, allowing water to pass through. The bedrock may have joints, also, for passage of water. If the water reaches a rock layer through which it cannot pass, it spreads to by-pass this impervious ("waterproof") layer. Zigzagging deeper and deeper, water finally reaches the water table—the level below which all spaces are full.

THE WATER TABLE

Take a glass and nearly fill it with sand. Add water. The water fills the spaces in the sand up to a certain level—the water table.

Earth's crust could be compared to the sand in the glass. In the glass the water table is

"Magic art" of dowsing—*Picture from a 17th-century book shows how location of water is indicated by a forked stick in hands of a dowser. Some people still believe in dowsing; few if any geologists do.*

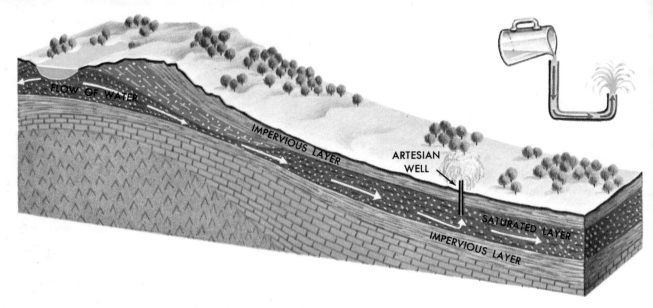

How an artesian well works—*Ground water moves downward between impervious (water-tight) strata (brown), which act as a pipe. The water gushes from the well pipe (lower right) because the top of the pipe is lower than the source of the water.*

nearly flat, but that is not usually so underground. The water table is likely to be uneven. Usually it is far below the surface in hills, much nearer the surface beneath valley bottoms. Also, there are likely to be scattered "hanging" water tables—places where a small area of impervious rock is holding water above the main table.

When the weather is rainy, more water goes underground and the water table rises. In dry times the table lowers. The water is always moving, seeking its level. If water does not keep coming down from above, the water table will sink to the level of the nearest stream.

Bedrock beneath the water table has varying amounts of space for water. Grains in shale and sandstone may be close-packed, and joints may be lacking; thus these rocks may contain little ground water. In limestone the joints are likely to have been enlarged by the dissolving action of ground water, so that considerable water may be held by this rock. Well-jointed basalt or granite also may have plenty of space.

Often we hear of underground "reservoirs." Caves full of water may exist in limestone but are rare in other bedrocks. When a well driller

speaks of a "reservoir" he is usually referring to a large amount of water held between soil or rock grains and within joints. Even in limestone, caves can exist only near the ground surface. Farther down, caves would be collapsed by pressure. At a depth of 2,000 feet in the crust pressure has closed up most joints and greatly reduced the spaces between rock grains. Few molecules penetrate to a mile.

WELLS SHALLOW AND DEEP

An old-fashioned well is simply a hole dug down below the water table, with the inside walled up to prevent cave-ins. For a modern

A water table—*Where the water table (upper border of pink zone) is above the land surface, there is a spring, brook, swamp, or lake. Beneath the water table, water fills all the spaces to which it can penetrate. Note the well that had to be abandoned because the water table went down below the well bottom.*

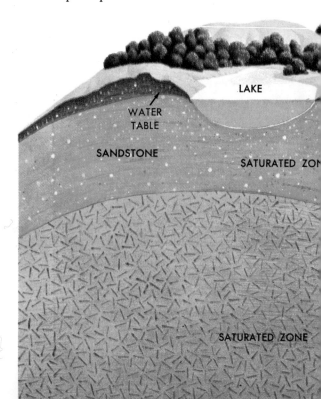

"driven" well a pipe with a perforated point is driven down. At the top of the pipe is attached a pump to raise the water. Operating the pump is like sucking on a soda straw.

Because of differences in climate, rock types, and arrangements of rock layers, there is more ground water in some places than in others. Before driving a well experts try to learn what the rock types and layer arrangements are.

Ground water usually has minerals dissolved in it. Bicarbonate of calcium or magnesium makes water "hard": soap will not make suds in it easily. In some regions, especially deserts, the mineral content of water may make it undrinkable. However, the right combination of minerals in water may give it a pleasant taste or some medicinal value.

Shallow wells tend to grow dry during droughts. They are easily polluted by dirty water during floods, or by sewage and other wastes from nearby houses, stores, and factories. For a more reliable, purer water supply, wells must be driven hundreds of feet deep.

Some deep wells are "artesian." The name comes from the region of Artois, France, where the first such wells in Europe were driven. A true artesian well does not require a pump to bring the water up: the water comes up by its own pressure. This happens because the bottom end of the well pipe is in water descending between slanting impervious rock layers from a place higher than the top of the pipe. Since the

water seeks its level, it rises in the pipe and comes out at the top. A well from which the water must be pumped is not truly artesian.

WATER SHORTAGES

In some regions, both humid and arid, water is being pumped out of the ground faster than rainfall is replacing it. Farms dry up; cities run short of water; drinking water may be sold by the gallon. Aqueducts must be built to bring water from distant mountains or large rivers.

As water is pumped out of the ground, or as lakes and swamps are drained, the soil settles. Openings in the bedrock below close up. The ground surface starts to sink, often unevenly. When this happens in a city, walls of buildings may crack, streets may buckle, and water and gas mains may break. These troubles have been serious in Mexico City. The sinking of ground beneath Venice, Italy, due to withdrawal of ground water for use by nearby factories, threatens to cause flooding of the city by the Mediterranean Sea.

LIMESTONE UNDERWORLDS

Limestone caverns demonstrate what water can do in dissolving rock underground. Consider the story of Mammoth Cave, Kentucky.

Some 225 to 275 million years ago, an arm of the Gulf of Mexico reached up into what is now the Midwest. For perhaps 30 million years it stayed there. Then the land rose and the sea

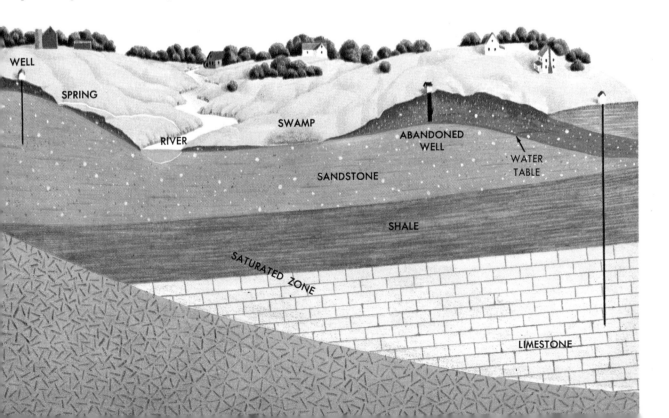

retreated, leaving a deposit of limestone covering thousands of square miles. This rock, as much as 1,200 feet thick in Kentucky, had formed from minerals in the water and limy remains of countless animals and plants.

For millions of years after the sea withdrew, the limestone was exposed to air and rain. Water percolated down through cracks. Carbon dioxide, entering the water from air and soil, gave the water the chemical ability to dissolve out the calcium carbonate, which makes up most of the limestone. Thus tunnels were made in the rock; they grew larger and larger, and some became caverns. Roofs over some caverns collapsed from the weight of overlying rock, but many caverns near the surface remained intact.

Mammoth Cave is one of the largest networks of tunnels and caverns so far discovered.

A sinkhole pond—*This 100-foot-deep specimen is one of several along a gypsum scarp in Bottomless Lakes State Park, New Mexico.*

Cross section of a sinkhole—*This hollow, made by descending rainwater, is seen in a Kentucky roadcut.*

Today, because the water table has fallen, we can explore the upper parts. Farther down, the tunnels and caverns are still under water.

Such caverns are found in regions where there are limestone layers high enough and well enough jointed so that water has been able to percolate down through them freely for thousands of years. These are the conditions that made many other fine limestone caverns, including Lehman Caves, Nevada; Wind Cave, South Dakota; and numerous caves in Virginia.

Carlsbad Caverns, New Mexico, is one of the world's largest exhibits of solution in limestone. The caverns are in the Guadelupe Mountains, carved from an enormous block of limestone—a reef—built up by coral animals in an ancient sea, long since vanished. The caverns originated perhaps ten million years ago and were enlarged during the Pleistocene Epoch, when there was more rainfall in New Mexico. Drying of the climate since then has lowered the water table, opening the caverns to view.

FAIRYLANDS IN STONE

Caverns contain many deposit features. These are made by precipitation of minerals from water dripping or flowing from ceilings and walls, and flowing over floors. Deposits of calcium carbonate are called travertine; those of calcium sulfate are gypsum. Deposition occurs in cave areas above the water table but wet with ground water seeping down from above.

Most familiar of deposit features is the stalactite. It starts as water drops slowly emerge from a small hole in a cave ceiling. Mineral in the water precipitates to form a ring of calcium carbonate around the hole. As more mineral is deposited, the ring gets longer, becoming a tube through which the water keeps trickling down. This tube is the stalactite.

Eventually the stalactite may get blocked. Then the water comes down the sides. In this way a stalactite may keep growing for hundreds, even thousands, of years.

Drip to the cave floor may produce stalagmites. These are somewhat like upside-down

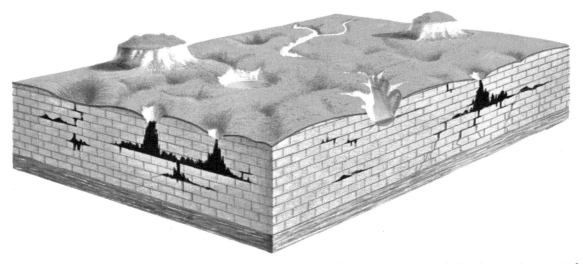

Limestone country—*If high enough for good drainage, a landscape on limestone bedrock may feature sink-holes, caverns, dry valleys, and underground streams—all typical of "karst" (limestone) topography.*

stalactites. A stalactite and a stalagmite may join to form a column or pillar.

One of the oddest of deposit features is the helictite, consisting of a thin, twisted tendril of calcium carbonate. Particularly beautiful are the crystals that build out from scattered pores in a ceiling; in a lighted cave they suggest fields of stars. Clusters of crystals may make elaborate "flowers."

Water flowing down cave walls may deposit travertine in long columns like organ pipes or waterfalls. Water flowing over a cave floor may produce travertine terraces. Forms suggesting scallops and lily pads also are common.

DISSOLVING THE LAND

Landscapes on limestone in humid regions tend to be destroyed by solution rather rapidly.

The land of the Mammoth Cave region is losing an amount of rock equal to about one foot of elevation each 2,000 years.

Some limestone landscapes are dotted with sinks. These are depressions, or holes, where rainwater streams run underground or where the ground has sunk over collapsed cave roofs. Here and there one may find a "lost river"— a stream that dives underground, perhaps to emerge again yards—or miles—away.

Elevated limestone landscapes may be underlain by miles and miles of tunnels. These are fascinating to "spelunkers," who explore the tunnels with flashlights and swimming gear. Some of these explorers become lost or get caught in narrow passages. Wise spelunkers always explore in groups with thoroughly experienced leaders.

Helictites in Mammoth Cave—*These tendrils of travertine grow probably by capillary action of solutions.*

Flowstone in Timpanogos Cave, Utah—*Minerals in water descending from holes in wall made columns.*

Lakes and Swamps

LAKES are among the pleasantest gifts of nature. They are beautiful to look at, fun to fish in, cool to swim in, breezy to sail on. They are homes for birds, fish, and other animals, not to mention attractive plants. They supply us with water. They give us a feeling of space in a crowded world.

Natural lakes are most common in areas that were covered with glacier ice during the Pleistocene Epoch—the ice age that ended only about 10,000 years ago. Lakes of glacial origin are scattered over the northern parts of North America, north and central Europe, and northern Asia. But lakes are otherwise rare as natural geological features. Erosion tends to destroy lake basins rather soon after they are made. That is why areas not glaciated during the Pleistocene, such as Africa and South America, have few natural lakes.

HOW LAKES COME TO BE

Essentially a lake is a body of water lying in a basin, or hollow, whose bottom is below the water table. Water finds its way into this basin by way of direct rainfall, surface streams, and springs. Most lakes receive more water than they can hold, and the excess escapes through an outlet—the lowest point on the basin's edge.

Land of lakes—*This broad lowland north of Ft. Yukon, Alaska, is thickly covered with rock ground off nearby mountains by glaciers, then washed down onto the lowland by swift streams. Blocking of stream channels by the sediment has produced many lakes.*

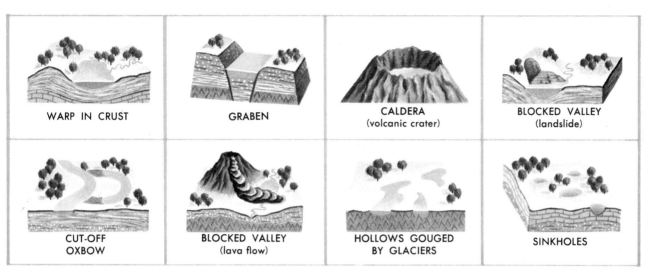

WARP IN CRUST	GRABEN	CALDERA (volcanic crater)	BLOCKED VALLEY (landslide)
CUT-OFF OXBOW	BLOCKED VALLEY (lava flow)	HOLLOWS GOUGED BY GLACIERS	SINKHOLES

Eight Kinds of Lake Basins

Everyone has heard of "bottomless" lakes, but none exist. All lakes have a bottom—if your line is long enough.

Famous lakes illustrate in different ways how basins are formed in nature. Beautiful Lake San Cristobal near Lake City, Colorado, is a lake created by the natural damming of a valley. It formed after the valley of the Lake Fork of the Gunnison River was blocked by the famous "Slumgullion" earthflow—an enormous mass of wet volcanic ash moving down from the San Juan Mountains. Damming of a valley can be done also by a landslide (such as the Gros Ventre slide), a lava flow, or a glacier.

Some lake basins form by the sinking of a crustal block. A chain of lakes of this kind extends 3,500 miles along the African Rift Valley, from Israel to Northern Rhodesia. Along the rift are the Sea of Galilee, the Dead Sea, the Red Sea, and Lakes Nyasa and Tanganyika. The latter has depths to 4,700 feet—approaching a mile.

Basins formed by sinking of crustal blocks hold the world's deepest lakes. Lake Baikal, in southeastern Siberia, is 5,710 feet deep—more than a mile. It is the world's deepest lake, with a bottom 4,226 feet below sea level and a volume of water calculated at 5,800 cubic miles —almost equaling the volume of all the Great Lakes together. A lesser lake on a sunken block is Lake Tahoe, on the California-Nevada border, 1,600 feet deep. Minor examples are the sag ponds along California's San Andreas fault.

Occasionally a meandering river, such as the Mississippi in Louisiana, floods over its banks and cuts off one of its oxbow loops. If the river deposits sand and silt so as to close the ends of the loop, a basin for an "oxbow lake" is thus created.

Every century or two Earth is struck by a meteorite that blasts a hole big enough to hold a lake. Recently geologists have been identifying many such basins, called "impact craters" or "astroblemes." Meteor Crater, in Arizona, 3,950 feet wide and 570 feet deep, is now dry but held a lake during the Pleistocene humid period. Chubb Crater, west of Ungava Bay in Quebec, Canada, nearly 2 miles wide, still holds a lake.

A sag pond—*Una Lake, south of Palmdale, Calif., lies in a chain of small basins made by earth movements along the San Andreas fault.*

A glacial lake—*At the foot of Mt. Chiwawa in Washington's Cascade Mountains is Lyman Lake. It lies in a basin gouged by glacial action and is now fed by meltwater from ice and snow on the mountains.*

Some lakes occupy old volcanic craters. A famous one is Crater Lake, in Oregon, occupying the crater of the extinct volcano Mt. Mazama.

In regions of soluble bedrock—limestone or gypsum—small lakes occupy some of the sinks. Kentucky and central Florida have many such lakes. The sinks form by collapse of cave roofs or by solution of bedrock where surface streams dive underground.

Among the most scenic lakes are those fed by melting mountain glaciers in Alaska, the Canadian Rockies, Switzerland, Norway, and other cold lands. Some basins were made by glacial erosion; others formed by the damming of valleys by masses of glacier-broken rock. (More about these glacial processes will be told later.) Lakes fed by melting glaciers usually have a remarkable turquoise color due to the presence of glacier-ground rock—"rock flour" —in the clear water.

Some mountain regions where glaciers do not exist now, or are very small, have lake basins obviously made by sizable valley glaciers. Examples include lakes in New England's White Mountains, New York's Adirondacks, Colorado's southern Rockies, and California's Sierra Nevada. Glacial basins in these areas were made in the Pleistocene.

The plains of Canada, of the United States from Maine to Minnesota, and of northern Europe and Asia show countless glacier-made basins. These were made not by mountain glaciers but by Pleistocene ice sheets thousands of feet thick. Basins were made in bedrock by glacier ice scraping rocks over it and pulling out

The Great Lakes: 11,000 B.C.—*Ice covers most of present area. Lakes drain west through Mississippi and east through Mohawk and Hudson river valleys.*

9,000 B.C.—*Mohawk Valley is now blocked by ice. Drainage therefore occurs southwestward from the old Lake Michigan basin to the Mississippi.*

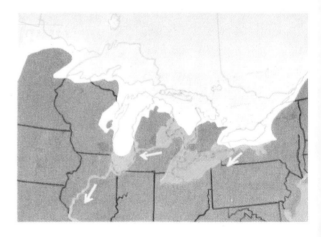

Carved by meltwater—*Sun Lake, Washington, lies in Grand Coulee, the long valley carved in the Columbia Plateau by water from the melting Pleistocene ice sheet. Note the huge potholes.*

chunks. Basins were shaped in sand and clay by ice movements or by sinking of earth around melting ice masses.

Cape Cod, an arm of Massachusetts running out into the Atlantic, is a mass of sand and clay left by ice melting at the end of the Pleistocene. Dotting the Cape are many freshwater ponds, occupying hollows called kettles. Kettles formed as the ground sank over buried blocks of melting ice. Kettles whose bottoms are now below the water table hold ponds.

Kettles and kettle ponds are likely to be seen wherever a large mass of glacier ice melted back, leaving thick deposits of rock waste. Such ponds are seen in the East as far south as New Jersey, and westward from New England to Wisconsin and Minnesota. The Canadian plains have numerous kettle ponds as well as rock-basin ponds.

THE GREAT LAKES

Most famous of all American bodies of water are the Great Lakes. These occupy five river valleys that originated millions of years ago. During the Pleistocene the valleys were enlarged by glacial erosion, then filled with meltwater as the last Pleistocene ice sheet decayed. Excess lake water, blocked by the ice to the north, drained southward to the Mississippi or eastward by way of the Mohawk River to the Hudson River in eastern New York.

The last Pleistocene ice sheet took centuries to melt. As its southern edge melted back into Canada, an arm of the Atlantic reached into the area to form the Champlain Sea. Into this sea

7,000 B.C.—*Melting of ice allows drainage westward through Lake Superior and east once more through the Mohawk and Hudson river valleys.*

6,000 B.C.—*Further melting of the ice sheet northward and rising of land to the south allow northeastward drainage (as today) through St. Lawrence Valley.*

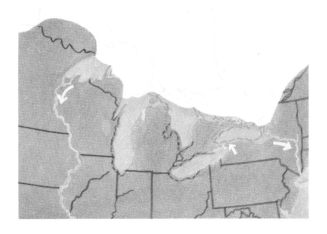

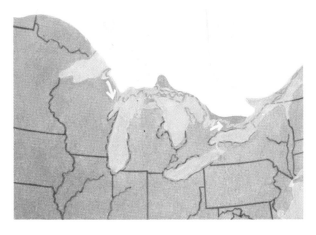

Where ice blocks melted—*These ponds near Monponsett, Massachusetts, are typical of many in the region. They lie in basins made by the sinking of sand and clay around blocks of melting Pleistocene ice.*

Erie, and Ontario to the St. Lawrence and the Atlantic Ocean.

The meltwater left in the Great Lakes by decay of the Pleistocene ice disappeared long ago. But there is plenty of rain now, and the lakes receive runoff water from surrounding lands with twice the area of the lakes. The lakes hold about 6,000 cubic miles of water—enough to fill a space 20 miles wide, 50 miles long, and 6 miles high. Lake Ontario pours 1½ to 2 million gallons into the St. Lawrence every second.

WHY LAKES DISAPPEAR

By geological standards, lakes are short-lived. If the climate becomes a little dryer, evaporation may take water out of a lake faster than it enters. A lake may fill with sediments washed or blown into it, or with remains of plants and animals that have lived in it. Or the basin may be eliminated and the water drained off by crustal movements.

Most lakes have an outlet for excess water. Flow through the outlet cuts it deeper and deeper, and so the lake level gradually lowers. Eventually the basin may become just a widening in a valley.

the ancestors of the Great Lakes drained. But this region which had been under mile-thick ice rose as the weight of the ice was removed. This uplift pushed back the sea. Now the lake water drained toward the Atlantic by way of the St. Lawrence Lowland, becoming the St. Lawrence River. And so was completed the chain by which water today travels east from Lakes Superior and Michigan through Lakes Huron,

How Niagara Gorge Could Empty Lake Erie (If Man Did Not Interfere)

Today—*Gorge reaches only to Niagara Falls.*

15,000 years from now—*Gorge is halfway to Buffalo.*

25,000 years from now—*Gorge empties Lake Erie.*

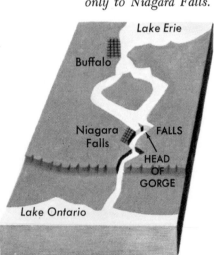

Making the most of a salt lake—*Workers in Colombia, South America, rake up salt for industrial use. Such lakes afford common salt and often other minerals such as borax, gypsum, and potash.*

All the Great Lakes are gradually filling with sediments. Lake Michigan is filling at the rate of three inches per 100 years—fast enough to fill in 250,000 years. If the climate should become dryer and the water level should fall, the 250,000 years might be cut in half. The same is true for the other Great Lakes.

There is another "threat." By erosion, the head of the Niagara River gorge is advancing toward Lake Erie at the rate of 4 or 5 feet per year. In about 25,000 years the gorge could reach Lake Erie and the lake could be emptied. Meanwhile the flow through the chain of lakes would speed up, connections between the lakes would be deepened by erosion, and the lakes would be converted into river valleys—as they were before the Pleistocene glaciers came.

Engineers can build dams to prevent emptying of the Great Lakes. Man-made dams are preserving countless lakes already.

Since the Pleistocene, giant bodies of water, such as Lake Bonneville, in Utah, and scores of lakes in the Southwest have shrunk or dried up entirely. Even the Great Lakes were once larger than they are now. Within the short span of human history, Lake Ngami in Africa has dwindled from an inland sea to a marsh. By their very nature, the so-called salt lakes—which make up 40 per cent of all—are "dying."

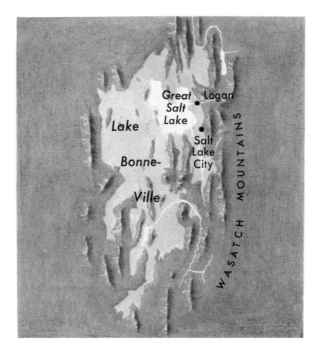

A dwindling giant—Lake Bonneville, in Utah, *was vast and deep toward the end of the Pleistocene ice age. Today it is Great Salt Lake.*

75

Among the few new lakes forming naturally in our time are those being created by sandbar formation along seacoasts and deltas. An example is Lake Pontchartrain, in Louisiana.

GREAT SALT LAKE'S ANCESTOR

The story of Lake Bonneville shows how an enormous lake—an inland sea—can fade away because of a change in climate.

Toward the end of the Pleistocene this lake, occupying the western half of what is now Utah, was as much as 1,000 feet deep. The climate was humid because of the melting of huge amounts of glacier ice. Streams were feeding the lake more water than it lost by evaporation and through its outlets.

With the close of the Pleistocene, the climate became dryer. The lake's level began to fall; its area shrank. Eventually the water level fell below the outlet level, so that no more water flowed out. Shrinkage of the lake area reduced the rate of evaporation. Thus, in our time, the lake can still exist.

Today shrunken Lake Bonneville is known as Great Salt Lake. It is only a third as large as old Bonneville, and its greatest depth is only about 12 feet. Around it are vast stretches of dry salt flats. On nearby mountain slopes are ancient shorelines—wave-cut terraces—as much as 1,000 feet above the present ones. The present lake has no outlet; it "needs" every drop of water that comes in via rainfall and streams. If the climate becomes just a little dryer for a period of years, the lake will dwindle to nothing.

FRESH WATER AND SALT

Lake Bonneville contained fresh water. Great Salt Lake is saltier than the sea. Why?

A trough lake—*Lower Ausable Lake, in New York's Adirondacks, lies in a valley deepened and widened into a "trough" by the action of Pleistocene glacier ice.*

A cypress swamp—*Here, near Lake Charles, Louisiana, the water table is slightly above ground level, and a swamp has formed. With a slight lowering of the water table the swamp would disappear.*

In glacial times rainwater and meltwater kept Bonneville fresh despite the salt brought in by streams from the mountains. After the glaciers melted away, the climate became dryer and the lake level sank below the outlet levels. Evaporation took water out of the lake without taking the salt, which was no longer escaping through the outlets. The lake became saltier and saltier.

Bonneville's story is not unusual. Shorelines and other traces of at least seventy-five salt lakes are found in the Great Basin—the dry region between Oregon and New Mexico, west of the Rockies. Most of these lakes were fresh during the Pleistocene. Salt lakes are common also in North Africa, Asia Minor, and central Asia. Largest are the Caspian and Dead seas.

SWAMPS AND MARSHES

Where the water table and the ground level are about the same, a swamp may form. A little dry weather may cause the water table to fall enough to let the swamp dry up. One heavy rain may make the swamp a shallow lake.

Some regions have vast swampy areas. In the lower Mississippi Valley a tremendous volume of water moves very near the surface. Thousands of square miles are swampy most of the year.

Famous in North America are the Everglades of Florida and the Dismal Swamp of North Carolina and Virginia. These lowlands were covered until a few thousand years ago by the ocean. As the land rose, the salt water drained away and fresh water from rainfall took its place. The swamps may vanish if the land rises a little more; or, if the land sinks, the sea will again move in. If the land sinks just enough to let the tides bring in sea water at intervals, the swamps will be salt marshes.

When drained, swamps make fertile land for farms and convenient sites for factories, docks, and residential developments. Draining is done by digging trenches to collect water and lead it away. Swamps are, however, important parts of our natural environment, and today in many regions they are being carefully preserved.

77

The Ways of Streams

WATER on Earth that is evaporated by the Sun's heat becomes clouds, which become rain and snow, which become water on and in the ground. Most of this water is moving in sheets and streams. It dissolves rock and decomposes it by chemical action. With sediments as abrasives it grinds bedrock. It transports rock waste from high places to low ones. Thus it shapes landscapes—sculpturing highlands, carving valleys, covering lowlands with sediment.

Through the ages erosion has lowered vast areas of the continents almost to sea level, again and again. Highlands exist today only because crustal forces have raised the crust while erosion has been grinding it down.

EARLY IDEAS

The ancients took rivers for granted. Most rivers, it seemed, had been created along with everything else at the beginning of the world. A river was simply water running over the land, following whatever valleys were handy. Scholars discussed where the water came from but didn't follow rivers back to the sources to find out for sure.

In the seventeenth century, Athanasius Kircher wrote that water rises underground into the hills, flows down in streams to the sea, leaks through the sea bottom, and—somehow—works back up into the hills again. No one in those days fully recognized the water cycle, which is simple in principle but not easy to witness. Also, the ancients had little understanding of ground water and how it feeds streams.

James Hutton, the Scottish farmer, was the first to recognize that most landforms are the handiwork of running water more than of any other geologic agent. His ideas stimulated later geologists to observe rivers carefully to see how they really "behave."

The most famous nineteenth-century investigator of rivers was John Wesley Powell of the U.S. Army. He was a naturalist and an

Indian expert as well as a geologist. Despite the loss of an arm in the Civil War he led several expeditions in the West, including a trip down the Colorado River from southern Wyoming to the western end of the Grand Canyon in Arizona. The expedition was baked by the sun, stung by windblown sand, tossed by rough

water, forced to portage again and again around rapids and waterfalls, and handicapped by losses of supplies and instruments. Three men who left the main party were killed by hostile Indians. Yet Powell found time to study the ever-changing river and its channel. For the first time a river was studied over a distance

The vigor of youth—*Among America's best-known streams is the Yellowstone, shown here in the zigzag valley it has cut through the soft red and yellow volcanic rocks of Yellowstone National Park. Highland valleys with swift streams like this are in what geologists call a youthful phase of development.*

of hundreds of miles, flowing narrow and wide, fast and slow, through plain and canyon, in soft rock and hard. In the Grand Canyon, Powell also inspected the most splendid display of sedimentary rocks on the continent—a billion-year record of Earth history.

THE TRAVELS OF WATER

Among all the wonders of the world none is greater than the travels of water.

Imagine a rocky mountainside—in Pennsylvania, let's say—where heavy rain is falling. A little rainwater is taken up by plants and soil. Some sinks underground. The rest runs over the ground, following chains of little depressions downward. These lead to small gullies, which lead to larger gullies.

Perhaps halfway down the mountain many gullies come together to make a ravine. This is so deep that its bottom is below the water table. Water from springs makes a brook in the ravine. Rainwater runs down little gullies in

the ravine's sides. The brook dashes down the mountain toward the valley bottom.

There the brook joins a larger stream—a small river already carrying the waters of a dozen brooks. This stream, a few miles farther on, reaches a bigger valley that contains water from fifty brooks—rainfall and ground water from a thousand square miles.

Thus the joining of the waters, all flowing seaward, goes on. A day after raindrops fall on the mountain in Pennsylvania some are swept into the rushing Allegheny. In another day they are in the mighty Ohio, sliding southwestward along the West Virginia border. Down they go, past Kentucky, past Indiana and Illinois, and in another week they are emptying into the Father of Waters—the Mississippi.

For perhaps ten days the raindrops follow the loops and turns of the Mississippi, working ever southward. At last, three or four weeks after they fell from the sky, Pennsylvania's raindrops, along with drops from thirty other states, covering 1,244,000 square miles, pour into the Gulf of Mexico.

THE MAKING OF VALLEYS

By definition, a valley is a long depression cut by stream action. Some depressions often called "valleys" are not true valleys. Such depressions include those made by crustal movements, by wind action on sands of deserts and beaches, by waves and currents along shores, and by the advance of glacier ice.

Pour a pailful of water slowly on soft, uneven ground. The water divides into separate streams, each following a chain of little depressions downslope. By lifting or dragging bits of sand or clay, the streams cut small channels. As more water is poured onto the ground, the channels are cut below ground level. They become what we call small valleys.

Everyone has seen deep gullies cut into a field by one hard rain. But where a stream is

A canyon-type valley—*Near Navajo Bridge, Arizona, the Colorado River cuts into the Colorado Plateau. The valley walls are steep mainly because in this dry climate downcutting is rapid relative to weathering, erosion, and mass wasting on the valley sides.*

running over bedrock, cutting is much slower. It is done mostly by abrasion—the scraping of bedrock by pieces of stone moved over it by the stream. A little cutting is done also as bits of the bedrock are decomposed or dissolved by the water.

In general, the rate of cutting by a stream depends on the velocity of flow and the resistance of the rock. The faster the stream and the lower the rock resistance, the more rapid is the cutting.

Deep valley cutting takes a long time. The cutting of the Grand Canyon a mile deep by the Colorado River has taken at least two million years, at the rate of no more than five or six inches per century—on the average—through moderately resistant rock layers. Cutting is even slower in strong bedrock, such as New England quartzite or Rocky Mountain granite.

Cutting is mostly downward, because it is done mainly by sediments grinding the streambed. But as a channel deepens, its sides tend to be undermined by stream action, so that rock material falls or slides down to the streambed —the process called mass wasting. Valley sides weather, and are eroded by rainwater and meltwater. Rock waste from mass wasting and erosion becomes sediment on the streambed—the "bedload."

Thus a valley is deepened and widened by three processes: downcutting by the stream, mass wasting and erosion on the valley sides, and removal of the rock waste.

Rough going—*Rapids like this in the Grand Canyon of the Colorado River were negotiated by Major Powell and his party in 1869. Brown with rock debris, the river here is cutting through sandstone.*

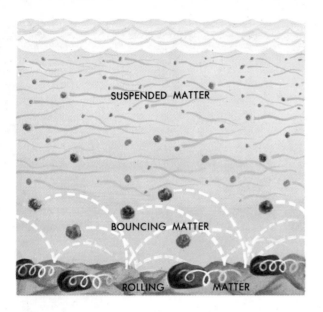

How a stream carries sediments—*When flow is fairly strong, the stream can carry silt (the smallest rock grains). Grains of sand and gravel are bounced along the bottom. When flow is strongest, cobbles and even boulders may be rolled.*

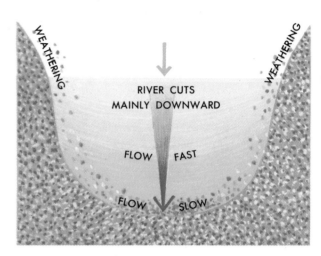

How a valley is cut—*Cutting by stream flow is mainly downward, deepening the valley. Valley widening results from the action of weathering, mass wasting, and erosion by sheets or streams of water on the valley sides.*

VALLEY PROFILES

Many valleys, seen lengthwise, have a V-shape. This is likely if the valley sides are on relatively weak rock which tends to loosen and slide down. V-valleys are common in lavas, sandstones, and shales.

Some valleys are of the canyon, gorge, or "slot" type, with nearly vertical walls. These are valleys in which mass wasting is slight relative to downcutting. Often the stream is following a deep fracture in the bedrock as it cuts down. Often, too, the stream is cutting into a very strong rock like granite.

ALCOVES, TUNNELS, AND NATURAL BRIDGES

Swift streams in narrow valleys create inter-esting sculptures. One is the alcove: a cave made by a stream in the valley side at a curve. Rounding the curve, water digs hard into the outside channel bank, undercutting it and making a wide cave—the alcove.

A swift stream in a meandering, or looping, gorge may cut through the bedrock wall that separates two sides of a loop. Thus a tunnel is made. The stream may now go through the tunnel, leaving the old roundabout watercourse dry. Later, as the land is lowered by erosion,

the tunneled wall is gradually destroyed. Part of it may remain for a time as a "natural bridge" —like Natural Bridge in Virginia and Rainbow Bridge in Utah.

LOST RIVERS

Some regions, such as Kentucky and southern Indiana, are known for their "lost rivers." These are streams that flow on the surface for a distance and then plunge underground—usually to appear again a few hundred yards or a few miles farther on. While on the surface such a stream is running over an insoluble rock layer. When it reaches soluble bedrock, it dives down into passages dissolved out by ground water. It flows underground, working downward, until it meets another insoluble layer. This layer leads the stream either to a "rise" (an opening at the ground surface) or to a zone of rock which allows it to go still deeper underground.

WATER GAPS AND WIND GAPS

A river valley cutting through a mountain ridge is called a water gap. Some gaps are made by gradual lengthening of ravines up mountain slopes. Thus, a ravine may lengthen up one side of a ridge all the way to the top, where it meets the head of a ravine on the

other side. Downcutting in the ravines on both sides may eventually slice through the ridge completely, forming the gap.

Other water gaps are made by what are called superposed streams. To understand, imagine a river flowing over a plain which is the surface of sediments that cover an ancient mountain ridge. As the region is lowered by erosion, the stream starts sawing into the buried ridge. By the time erosion has removed most of the sediments covering the ridge, the stream has sliced through it to make the gap.

Water gaps like this are common in the Appalachians and Rockies. In the past, these ranges have been eroded low, covered with sediments, then uplifted and sliced with new valleys.

A valley between ridges in a mountain range may lengthen upstream until it meets a water gap. Often the stream in the lengthwise valley is following a band of relatively weak rock and thus has cut lower than the water gap. So, when it reaches the gap, it "captures" the stream in the gap; that is, the stream in the gap is diverted into the lengthwise valley because this has a lower bottom. The gap goes dry, becoming what is called a wind gap. Such gaps are common in old mountain ranges which, like the Appalachians, consist of long rock folds.

VALLEY SYSTEMS

Now and then a new land surface is made—such as a sea bottom raised to become land, or an area covered by lava flows. Streams follow paths along hollows in the new surface, cutting valleys and thus starting the development of a drainage system.

Thanks to a resistant layer—*Splendid Niagara Falls, like many other falls, has formed where a stream flows over the edge of a resistant rock layer and undermines it by eroding weaker layers beneath.*

An alluvial fan—*Rock waste transported down a highland valley, usually by a swift but temporary stream, may spread out on the lowland as a fan. This fan in Death Valley is typical of many in arid regions.*

Stream capture, or "piracy," is important in the development of the system. By headward erosion (erosion toward their heads) valleys connect. At each connection running water turns into the lower valley. Thus over long periods many connections are made and drainage becomes more efficient.

Development of an efficient system over a wide area takes millions of years. In the early stage, valleys are widely spaced, with broad, flat areas between them. These areas separating streams are called divides. Gradually the valleys multiply, the divides grow narrower, the land becomes rugged. But as the land is lowered by erosion, valleys widen into plains and highlands shrink, and the landscape becomes gently rolling.

FANS, CONES, AND BRAIDS

A stream rushing down a steep slope is powerful enough to transport not only sand and gravel but cobbles and perhaps boulders. But when the stream reaches the valley bottom, its power to move this bedload suddenly wanes. Thus at the foot of a mountain ravine there is often a mass of "stalled" bedload spreading out fanlike over the valley bottom. Such deposits are called alluvial fans (or "cones" if they slope steeply). They are noticed especially in arid regions, where there is little vegetation to slow the descent of rock material or to cover fans that do form.

On some valley floors a stream divides into many interconnecting channels, separated by long, narrow islands of sediment. This phenom-

Anatomy of Niagara Falls—*Beneath are alternating layers of hard and soft rock. The present falls is maintained by the hard top layer. Dotted lines show possible future profiles of the falls as the river cuts deeper.*

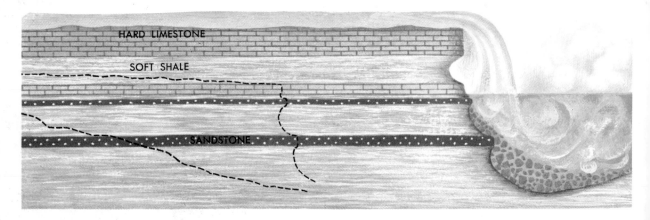

HARD LIMESTONE

SOFT SHALE

SANDSTONE

A natural bridge—*Rainbow Bridge, in southern Utah, is the remnant of a tunnel cut by stream action.*

enon is called braiding because it may suggest the look of braided hair. Braiding occurs where sediments are coarse and resist the flow, causing the stream to spread out and divide into many channels to get through.

Braiding is common in northern Canada and Alaska, where valleys have deep deposits of coarse rock waste from melting glacier ice.

WHY WATERFALLS?

Cliffs for waterfalls have various origins.

Some cliffs form as crustal blocks shift up or down. At Africa's great Victoria Falls the water plunges 420 feet into a graben—a depression formed by the sinking of a block. In Utah's Wasatch Mountains and Wyoming's Tetons, streams pour over cliffs formed by the rise of mountain blocks.

During the Pleistocene, mountain glaciers deepened many major valleys, cutting off the ends of tributary valleys and leaving them "hanging." Today there are fine waterfalls from many of these hanging valleys—for example, Bridalveil Falls in Yosemite.

Most waterfalls owe their existence to a resistant rock layer overlying a weaker layer. An example is Niagara Falls. As the Niagara River reaches the falls, it is flowing over a layer of resistant limestone. Under this are relatively weak shale and sandstone. Falling water dashes against the cliff, eroding the weak rock faster than the limestone. The limestone layer hangs out over the layers below, keeping the cliff steep. Now and then an overhang breaks off, more soft rock is eroded out, and a new overhang is made. In this way the cliff is kept steep and retreats upstream.

Niagara Falls is retreating toward Lake Erie at the rate of four or five feet per year. But even if this process is left to nature, the falls will never reach Lake Erie. When the falls is

Meanders on a floodplain—*Alaska's Christian River seeks the path of least resistance along a wide valley bottom. Several oxbow lakes and many meander scars are visible.*

about two miles upstream from where it is now, the river will have cut through the limestone into shale. Overhangs will no longer develop. The cliff will become a gentle slope, with rapids instead of falls.

Another process, too, is threatening the falls. The limestone layer is much cracked. Blocks are falling more frequently to the base of the falls. So much water is now being taken from the river for power plants that the water going over the falls is not enough to erode away the fallen rock. If present conditions continue, the heap of fallen rock will rise high enough against the cliff to convert the falls into a rapid.

FLOODPLAINS

In broad valleys, streams may overflow their banks and deposit alluvium—that is, stream-transported sediments—widely over the valley floor. The level surface of the alluvium is called a floodplain.

A river on a floodplain shifts from side to side as if trying to find a way through the sediments, which may be many yards deep. Individual loops of the stream are called meanders. During a flood, rushing waters may cut across from one loop to another, making a new channel called a cutoff. In this way old meanders tend to be abandoned as new ones develop.

The ends of an abandoned meander may become dammed by flood sediments, so as to form an oxbow lake. Eventually this may fill with sediments and become a "meander scar."

From the human viewpoint, floods are often disastrous. Rampaging waters drown farmers' fields, wash out highways and bridges, sweep away houses and other buildings. However, silt spread by flooding, mixed with organic wastes, makes fertile soil for which farmers and gardeners are grateful.

As barriers against floodwaters, levees are built along the sides of a river. Levees are ridges of earth a few feet or yards high. In a flood, much of the sediment carried by the overflowing waters is deposited near the river channel to make "natural levees."

With each flood, the streambed and the levees may be built up further by deposition of more sediment. Eventually they may rise high above the floodplain. Then a levee break can allow serious flooding of the surrounding countryside.

The Mississippi Delta—*Here the Father of Waters deposits sediments from a million square miles.*

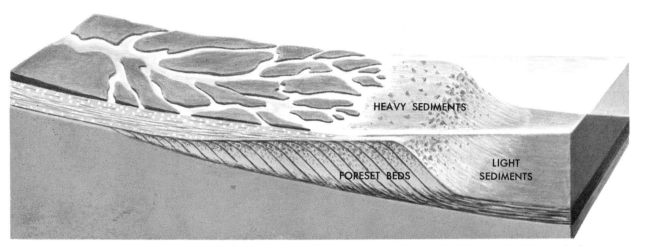

How a delta grows—*In each flood the river deposits a new layer of sediments (a foreset bed) at the delta's edge. Relatively light sediments are carried out to the delta's edges and beyond.*

HOW DELTAS FORM

As river water flows into a lake or a sea, it slows and deposits its bedload. The heaviest sediments are let down first, the lightest last. The tiniest particles—silt and organic wastes—do not sink until the water has virtually stopped moving—in a quiet bay or cove, or perhaps miles out on the sea bottom.

If the lake or sea bottom at the mouth of a river is not too deep, sediments piling up there may have a form like the Greek letter Δ, delta. That is what the deposit is called, although some deltas may be shaped more like a fan or a hand with spread fingers.

A delta may keep growing for thousands of years. Meanwhile the water keeps channels open all the way to the delta's outer edges. In flood periods water overflowing the river banks makes new side channels called distributaries leading to the delta's margins.

Mixed with rock waste in a delta are quantities of plant and animal waste. These make the delta fertile—a likely place for rich farms.

THE RIVER THAT MADE A STATE

Each year the Mississippi dumps onto its delta around 140 million tons of dissolved minerals, 400 million tons of sand and silt carried by the water, and 60 million tons of rock material that has been moved along the bottom. Great river systems such as the Mississippi's last for tens of millions of years. So we can appreciate what "erosion of the continents" means. Every continent except Antarctica has such systems.

That part of the Mississippi Delta south of Baton Rouge, Louisiana, results from perhaps ten million years of deposition. It may be five to six miles deep. This depth is not obvious, because the weight of the deposits has caused the bottom of the Gulf of Mexico here to sink.

87

A few thousand years are only a moment in the life of the Mississippi. This great artery may be as much as 20 million years old. Again and again it has changed course in its broad valley. During the Pleistocene it carried glacial meltwaters from the Great Lakes to the Gulf. But the Mississippi once flowed faster and more rapidly than today. Its bed is now being lowered by erosion about a foot every 5,500 years.

The present delta was begun only after the river had filled in an old bay covering the area that is now Louisiana. Residents can say that they owe their state to the river.

EGYPT'S BREADBASKET

The delta of Africa's Nile River is the most famous of all. At this delta ends the great river that begins 4,000 miles to the south in Uganda. The delta, covering 15,000 square miles, made possible the great civilization of ancient Egypt.

In the fifth century B.C. the famous Greek historian and traveler Herodotus visited Egypt and was fascinated by this land which had al-ready been civilized for twenty centuries. He explored the delta afoot and by boat. He studied accounts of the annual floods and discussed the delta with Egyptian priests, who were the learned men of that country. In his *Histories* Herodotus calculates that formation of the delta took 10,000 to 20,000 years—a figure very close to modern scientific estimates!

During the past thousand years Egypt's coastal region has sunk. Part of the old delta is now covered by the sea, but a vast expanse is still being farmed.

VALLEYS YOUNG AND OLD

Through geologic time, valleys may develop from "youth" through "maturity" to "old age."

Typical of young valleys are gullies and ravines on mountainsides. These zigzag and have steep sides and narrow bottoms. The bottoms may be bare rock, with potholes and a bedload of boulders and cobbles. Brooks are swift and interrupted by waterfalls, rapids, and pools.

A young valley usually leads down to a mature valley, deeper and wider. Long erosion

Mature dignity—*The valley of Germany's Rhine River is mature in this region south of Cologne. Note small floodplain at right; also groins built at curve to prevent further erosion of undercut slope.*

An Alaskan fiord—*Glacier Bay is an old river valley deepened by glacial action. As the glacier ice melted, the valley was invaded by ocean water.*

has straightened this older valley and smoothed its bottom, eliminating waterfalls, rapids, and pools. Lowering of the valley by downcutting has reduced its gradient (steepness of downslope); hence the stream is slower. Slower flow means slower downcutting, but erosion of the valley sides continues as before; hence the valley is widening fast relative to the rate of deepening. At some places the stream occupies only a narrow strip along the valley floor; there is dry ground between channel and valley wall.

In the mature valley, long streamwork has reduced boulders and cobbles to gravel, sand, and silt. The stream, being slower, is less efficient in moving this material. Sediment collects on the streambed, covering the bedrock; it accumulates between the valley wall and the channel. At flood time the stream speeds up and carries sediment downstream, but this is replaced by more material from upstream. This stream obviously does more transportation and deposition than downcutting.

Braiding in an Alpine valley—*Meltwater from Pré de Bar Glacier divides into many channels as it flows through glacial rock debris in Val Ferret, northern Italy. View is south from Grand Col de Ferret.*

A mature valley may lead down to a still older valley, very wide relative to its depth. The stream winds lazily in a narrow channel across the floodplain. The valley floor has been so much lowered by erosion that the stream has little gradient and little downcutting power. Streamwork consists mostly of transportation and deposition, as in the lower Mississippi Valley.

When very old a valley may be miles wide and the walls only a few score feet or yards high. The walls may, however, be about as steep as they were when the valley was young.

Waterfalls from hanging valleys—*These scenic examples are at Avalanche Lake, Glacier National Park.*

Along a river's course, stages of valley development vary. Traveling across country we may see a valley in young, mature, and old stages—in any order—within a few miles.

How old can a valley get? Downcutting can continue as long as there is a slope for the water to run down. Any valley floor can be lowered as long as it remains even slightly above sea level. The sea is considered to be "base level"—the lowest level to which land can be eroded by running water. Geologists speak also of "local" base level, which is the level of the lowest land in the region being considered.

"ACCIDENTS" TO VALLEYS

Valley development from youth to old age can be interrupted in various ways.

A landslide into a valley can dam a stream, causing it to form a lake. This rises until the water is high enough to find an outlet. Valley damming can be done by a lava flow, also.

Crustal movements may cause a valley floor to sink. Then the stream loses gradient and some or all of its power to cut down. Or a valley floor may be lifted so high that the stream is shifted into another valley.

Often, uplift simply gives a stream increased gradient and, therefore, greater power to cut down. Geologists call such a stream "rejuvenated," or made young again. If such a stream is in a wide valley, rejuvenation may cause it to start cutting a narrow gorge—a young valley—in the old valley floor. Examples of rejuvenated streams and their gorges are common on the Colorado Plateau because this region has been broadly uplifted during the past few million years.

During the Pleistocene, many valleys became occupied by glaciers. These interrupted stream-work and eroded the valleys vigorously, enlarging them and smoothing their sides.

When a coast sinks or sea level rises, sea water invades the coastal valleys. If these have low gradients, sea water may travel far inland, as in the Chesapeake Bay area. Mouths of these valleys are called estuaries.

Youth—*Uplift steepens the gradient of a stream. Flow speeds up. The valley is narrow and irregular, with pools and waterfalls. Tributaries, if any, are few.*

Early maturity—*Erosion has lowered the valley bottom. The valley is wider, with more tributaries. Sediments are accumulating on parts of valley bottom.*

A rejuvenated stream—*Once Utah's San Juan River meandered lazily over a plain. As uplift of the Colorado Plateau speeded the flow, the meander loops were cut deep, like this "gooseneck" near Mexican Hat.*

Even a change of climate influences valley-shaping. If rainfall increases, a stream's cutting power increases—if conditions otherwise remain the same. If less rain falls, cutting power wanes and the valley tends to clog up with stalled sediments.

Dry areas of the West have many valleys that were cut toward the end of the Pleistocene, when huge amounts of glacier ice were melting farther north and the climate was rainy. Most of these streams are today only a trickle or have disappeared entirely.

Later maturity—*The valley is still wider, its bottom lower. Tributaries are fewer. The topography is gentler. The stream has developed a floodplain, along which it meanders.*

Old age—*The land has been eroded almost to a plain. The original topography is gone. The stream meanders over a very wide plain. There are many abandoned loops, some with oxbow lakes.*

91

Realms of Ice

THE higher slopes of most big mountain ranges —the Alps, the Canadian Rockies, the Himalayas, and others—are white with snow all year. In deep mountain hollows the snow does not blow or melt away; it may become several hundred feet deep. On top the snow is soft, but underneath it is harder-packed, because of the weight on it. Toward the bottom of the deeper hollows, pressure has turned older snow—decades or centuries old—into hard pellets and solid masses of ice.

That ice is rock—real rock that happens to melt at a lower temperature than other kinds of rock. It is hard and stiff and strong; but even as rock it cannot resist the weight of hundreds of tons of snow and ice above. It bulges at the bottom like a mudpie. It squeezes over the edge of the hollow and moves down the mountainside—as a glacier.

Scientists have argued for a century about how glacier ice moves. Most agree that the glacier's own weight causes the ice pellets to roll, the ice crystals to bend and slip against each other, and the ice blocks to slide. Also, as pressure causes some of the ice to melt, the water moves to where there is less pressure, and refreezes there. Thus glacier ice moves.

GLACIER ICE: ROCK DESTROYER

A glacier is a rock destroyer whose work begins in the mountain hollow. From time to time the glacier ice freezes to the rock walls of the hollow and then breaks loose, plucking out chunks of rock. Centuries of plucking, along with frost weathering, enlarges the hollow into a rounded half-bowl called a cirque.

Squeezing over the threshold, or edge, of the cirque, glacier ice usually follows a valley

Terminus of a glacier—*Columbia Glacier, one of Alaska's finest, receives ice from scores of tributary glaciers. At the Pacific shore its front is approximately 5 miles wide and 200 feet high.*

down the mountain. On the way it is vastly more destructive than any river. Shoulders of bedrock in the valley are rammed, yanked, and broken as the ice goes by. Rock fragments from the valley walls and bottom are dragged along as scrapers to deepen and widen the valley.

CREVASSES, ICEFALLS, AND THE GLACIAL RIVER

Glaciers usually have many deep cracks, called crevasses. When the ice comes to a hump, it moves over stiffly, and the bending strain breaks the glacier's back into rows of crosswise crevasses. Where the valley widens, the ice spreads to fill the space, opening up lengthwise crevasses. Diagonal crevasses are made by strains resulting from the greater speed of the ice flow in midstream than at the sides.

Here and there the ice moves over a dip in the valley. An enormous squeezing force develops in the glacier's back, and a stretching force in its bottom. More breakage results.

When the ice comes to a rock step, or small cliff, it goes over as an icefall of broken blocks. Below the icefall the ice piles up, most of the blocks freeze together, and the flow continues to lower levels.

During warmer spells some glacier ice melts. The water runs down through crevasses and meltholes to the valley floor beneath the glacier, forming a stream there. The stream rushes through its blue ice tunnel, tumbling glacier-ground rock waste along with it.

TRIBUTARY GLACIERS

On its way down, the ice of a large valley glacier may be joined by ice of tributary glaciers. With much cracking and grinding the

Valley glaciers on Mt. Blanc, French Alps—*Snow-filled cirques and crevassed ice tongues are seen; also "horn" peaks and arêtes (knife-edge ridges), formed as erosion narrows divides between glaciers.*

tributary ice pushes in beside the mainstream and moves along with it, without mixing. Each tributary adds its load of moraine, or rock waste, to the trunk (main) glacier. Thus a trunk glacier may acquire many dark "stripes."

GLACIER'S END

The enemy of all glaciers is heat. Sunlight and warm air melt the ice. Also some ice evaporates directly into the air. Melting and evaporation, together called ablation, increase as glacier ice descends to warmer elevations. Eventually the ice reaches a level where ablation occurs as fast as ice arrives. There the glacier ends.

The lower end of a glacier is known as its terminus. (The word "snout" or "toe" also is used.) Over a period of years during which annual snowfall is relatively heavy, the terminus is farther down the valley than when the snowfall is lighter.

In warm seasons the ice at the terminus is soft and crumbling. From beneath it rushes a

torrent of meltwater, which will be milky-looking if it is loaded with ground-up rock—"rock flour." Reaching the lowland, the stream spreads out rock waste as "glacial outwash."

PIEDMONT GLACIERS AND ICE CAPS

In some polar and subpolar lands glacier ice does not melt before it reaches broad low-

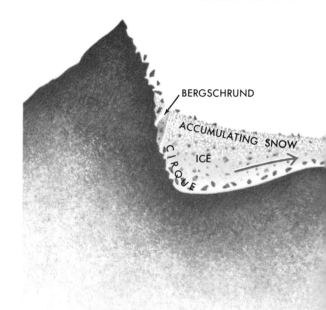

Ice fantasy—*The meltwater stream beneath Paradise Glacier, on Mt. Rainier in Washington, has carved this fantastic chamber as part of its tunnel.*

lands. There many glaciers may merge to make a piedmont (French: "foot-of-the-mountain") glacier. This gigantic ice mass may spread over tens of square miles. Such glaciers are seen in Alaska, Greenland, and Antarctica. Alaska's Malaspina Glacier is 40 miles wide.

In these areas, and in Norway as well, "ice caps" are seen. An ice cap is a broad, thick mass of snow and ice that covers or nearly covers a group of mountain peaks. From the cap's edges long tongues of ice creep down toward the lowlands.

A valley glacier—*Diagram shows how ice forms in a cirque, grinds downward through its valley, and dies away at warmer levels below. At far right, icebergs are formed where the glacier reaches the sea.*

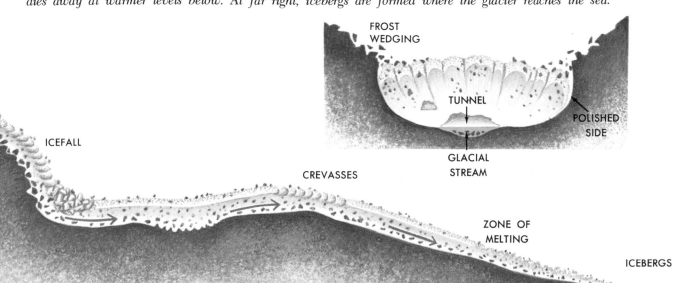

FROST WEDGING

TUNNEL

POLISHED SIDE

GLACIAL STREAM

ICEFALL

CREVASSES

ZONE OF MELTING

ICEBERGS

TERMINAL MORAINE

Glacial boulders in New York's Hudson Highlands—*Called "erratics," these were carried by a Pleistocene glacier and deposited on a glacier-smoothed hilltop.*

A kame in northern New Jersey—*This hillock, now being used for a sand quarry, consists of rock waste washed off glacier ice by a meltwater stream.*

ICE OVER ALL:
CONTINENTAL GLACIERS

In Greenland and Antarctica, mountains are covered with snow and ice all year. Ice moving down from the heights joins other ice streams to cover the lowlands as wide-spreading ice sheets. These masses, called continental glaciers, keep spreading until they reach the ocean. There, moving out into the water, the ice is buoyed up, and the bending strain causes chunks to break off. These are moved out to sea by wind, waves, and currents and are seen by ship and aircraft travelers as icebergs.

Soundings indicate a maximum depth of about 10,000 feet for the Greenland ice sheet, which covers about five-sixths of the island's 840,000 square miles. A few strips of seacoast remain open.

Antarctica's glacier buries all the land except for the higher mountains, which project above the ice. The ice covers 5,400,000 square miles to depths as great as 14,000 feet. Under the weight of the ice, parts of the continent have sunk below sea level.

THE AGES OF ICE

It is natural to suppose that glaciers have always been about what they are today. But geologists know otherwise.

In the year 1837 a young Swiss zoologist, an expert on fishes and a hiker with a sharp eye, delivered a historic lecture before the Helvitic Society, a scientific organization in Switzerland. With a very certain air he announced that glaciers of today hardly compare with those of the recent geologic past. Not so long ago, said Louis Agassiz to his unbelieving audience, ice sheets spread to cover lands as far south as central Europe and Asia.

Where had Agassiz picked up such a notion? It sounded more like imagination than science.

The year before, in the Alps, two friends had shown Agassiz polished and grooved bedrock—a tell-tale sign of glacier action—in valleys where,

A cirque in Scotland's Grampians—*These mountains show many hollows where Pleistocene glaciers developed. This one is near Dalmally. In the foreground is a plain on glacial outwash—sand and gravel.*

according to town records, no glaciers had ever been known. First with casual interest, then with excitement, Agassiz had climbed to existing glaciers to see how they formed, advanced, and melted, and then had examined the iceless slopes of the valleys below. Any doubts had quickly faded. Yes, ice had filled these quiet green valleys of central Europe. It must also have covered the lands to the north!

The response of scientists to Agassiz's report was "Nonsense!" But, as with Guettard and Desmarest (who had insisted on the volcanic nature of the Auvergne hills in France), the last word was with those who could show overwhelming evidence. That evidence was scattered all over central and northern Europe: not only polished and grooved rock but cirques, valleys with U-shapes and smoothed sides, boulders carried far from their places of origin, and heaps of glacial rock waste (called "drift").

Agassiz later went to America. During his distinguished twenty-seven years of teaching at Harvard he found time to explore areas of North America where, as in Europe, giant hands of ice had worked to shape the land.

THREE MILES THICK?

More than a century has passed since Agassiz shocked the Helvitic Society. Since then the story of past ice ages—there have been several—has been carefully pieced together.

The most recent glacial periods occurred during the past few million years. At least four different times, great domes of ice built up on the northern parts of North America, Europe, and Asia. Over thousands of years they spread southward, then melted back. When the climate was coldest, ice covered all Canada and reached south in long tongues as far as where St. Louis, Missouri, stands today. The average thickness of the ice in the north was a mile, and the flow down the Mississippi Valley has been estimated by some geologists as two to three miles deep. In the West there were mountain glaciers as far

Glacial "signatures"—*Rocks embedded in glacier moving in direction away from camera made long grooves in the bedrock, curved fractures, and gouges (curved hollows where chips broke out).*

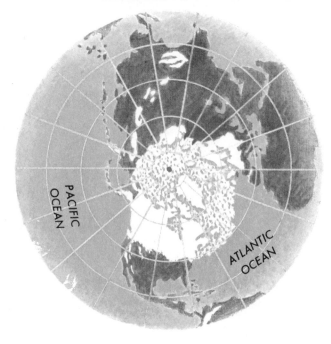

The great ice sheets—*Areas in white on the map were covered with ice during the Pleistocene Epoch.*

plains. It flattened forests, obliterated rivers, and forced wildlife to retreat before it.

Along the glacier's southern edges, beneath blue ice cliffs, in the shadows of evergreen forests, life went on as in polar lands today. Where Chicago and Philadelphia now stand, the musk-ox grazed on bleak meadows and drank from icy streams. Nearby roamed mammoths and mastodons, the great royal bison, and wild horses. Animals being exterminated included the camel, the ground sloth, the sabertooth cat, and the great wolf.

Northern Europe and Siberia saw the same drama of advancing ice and retreating wildlife. Along the ice margins lived mastodon and mammoth, reindeer and woolly rhinoceros, and giant cave bear. Fleeing south were tapir, rhinoceros, elephant—hosts of beasts that had thrived in a warmer Europe. Their descendants live in southern Asia and Africa today.

south as New Mexico. From Alaska to Lower California, from Greenland to Cuba, the ocean may have been dotted with icebergs.

As the continental glacier inched southward it sliced off tips of hills and gouged 60 to 70 feet of soil and bedrock out of the Canadian

A glacial trough in New Hampshire—*Erosion by a trunk (main) glacier gave Crawford Notch this U-shape, typical of strongly glaciated valleys. Ridges that formerly projected out into the valley were shaved off, leaving the valley sides relatively smooth.*

Left by a glacier—*Cape Cod consists of rock waste deposited at an ice sheet's southern edges. Ocean and wind are reshaping the huge mass of clay, sand, and gravel. The view is north over the Truro dunes.*

THE HAIRLESS HUNTER

Among the creatures that faced the looming ice in northern Europe and Asia were a group of clever newcomers in the animal world. Along the ice fronts these almost hairless, brown-skinned creatures hunted reindeer and mammoth with spears. They used fire, painted remarkable pictures in caves, and buried their dead. Learning in ways beyond ordinary animals, these early men thrived in the cold and became masters of the planet.

Perhaps just before the last glacial advance, some 35,000 years ago, men of northeast Asia wandered onto a strip of land leading to Alaska. Over they went. Plodding south, they found a path between partly melted ice domes. Today we dig up their spearpoints and campfire remains in Southwestern caves and streambeds.

THE LAST RETREAT

As the ice melted back, new forests grew up and animals moved north to take over the land once more. But the marks of ice were still there, and would be for millennia to come.

In central Canada and from Minnesota to Maine, glacial lakes filled thousands of hollows gouged in bedrock by glacier ice or shaped in glacial rock waste as the ice melted. Soil and rock scraped off Canada and carried south by the ice lay strewn scores of feet deep over the central United States, preparing rich land for farmers of our time.

On the East Coast a 100-mile-long ridge of clay, sand, and gravel showed where an ice front melted. We call that ridge Long Island. Farther north, dwindling ice had deposited heaps of rock waste now known as Cape Cod, Martha's Vineyard, and Nantucket. North of a line running from New Jersey to Missouri and thence north to Montana, hillocks and sheets of glacier-ground rock, with scatterings of boulders, mark the melting places of other glacier ice.

Today in Canada snow and ice last all year only in Labrador and the western mountains. To the east the Greenland ice sheet remains, feeding icebergs to the Atlantic. In the United States glaciers are seen only as far south as the Teton Range in Wyoming and the Sierra Nevada in California—and these are little ones. The Alps still have about 1,200 living glaciers, but most are small, and the piedmont type has disappeared.

Valley glaciers descending from the Greenland ice sheet—*These "outlet" glaciers, in northwest Greenland, are discharging into Bessels Fiord, which is full of sea ice. At right is the ice sheet.*

WILL THE ICE COME BACK?

Not only science-fiction writers, but geologists too, consider a new ice age possible. The record of the rocks shows that Earth has seen many glacial ages. One may suppose that conditions which brought on the Pleistocene "chill" could occur again—and probably will.

Over recent centuries Earth's climate has been warming. Glaciers have been gradually shrinking, the melting has been raising sea level, and average annual temperatures have been going up. However, since about 1950 the trend has been the other way. Scientists are wondering whether this cooling will continue or be reversed. Some have suggested that we live in an interglacial period—a period between continental glacier advances. If so, it is only a matter of time before much of the civilized world is covered with ice—unless man finds a way to hold it back.

Just what causes ice ages is still a matter of argument. The fall in average Earth temperature that brought on the Pleistocene was no more than about 11 degrees Fahrenheit. Such a drop could result from a relatively slight decrease in the Sun's heat output—not much more than ordinarily occurs during times of strong sunspot activity. Or it could result from an increase in the dust content of our atmosphere. Atmospheric dust increases in periods of heightened volcanic activity.

Another influence may be the widespread uplift of lands to form mountains. Mountains mean more snowfall and more glacier ice. Uplifts were considerable during the Pleistocene.

Still another explanation is crustal movements that change the circulation of ocean water. Some geologists think a sagging of the floor of the North Atlantic at the start of the Pleistocene caused an increased flow of southern water into the Arctic Ocean. This warming melted much arctic ice, exposing more of the Arctic Ocean to evaporation. Arctic air thus became more moist, more snow fell on northern lands, and glaciers therefore spread—or so the theory suggests.

Man's own activities could help to bring on a new glacial age. The burning of huge amounts of fuel and other materials has been adding gases and dust to the atmosphere. These could in time block enough solar heat to allow glaciers to grow and spread widely.

But some scientists take a contrary position. They say dust and dirt in the atmosphere reduce radiation of Earth's own heat into outer space. Still further, large quantities of carbon dioxide produced by burning spread over the planet as a kind of "window," allowing sunlight to enter and trapping it as a greenhouse does. Thus, they conclude, man's activities could prevent—not bring on—an ice age.

Oddly, continued melting of the world's glaciers could make a crisis of another sort. About 3¼ million cubic miles of water is now locked up in glacier ice—most of it in the Antarctic sheet, which covers millions of square miles. If all the planet's ice melted, the oceans would rise perhaps 300 feet, drowning vast areas of inhabited lowlands, including New York, Paris, London, and other important coastal cities.

A final answer to the question of why ice ages occur is unlikely in the near future. Probably not one cause, but many, are responsible. Some day ice sheets may start growing and spreading again, and then we shall have the answer—maybe.

Studying a glacier—*From Antarctica to north polar regions, glaciers are studied by enterprising geologists. Here a party is encamped on Juneau Icefield in Alaska.*

Deposited in water—*The clays of South Dakota's Badlands were deposited on the beds of streams and lakes some 40 million years ago. This dry but deeply gullied region of sedimentary rocks is rich in fossils.*

New Rocks from Old

WEATHERING, mass wasting, and erosion subject Earth's crust to continuing destruction. But along with this destruction there is construction also: the creation of the sedimentary rocks. These form from accumulations of disintegrated older rock and other mineral wastes.

The making of sedimentary rocks occurs very slowly, and mostly below ground or under water. We can see rock debris scattered on hillsides, and we can make wells scores of feet deep in the sediments of valley bottoms, but the actual conversion of rock materials into new rock is rarely visible. No wonder the origin of the sedimentary rocks became part of scientific knowledge only in recent times.

Several ancient Greek philosophers, including Anaximander, who lived in the seventh century B.C., noticed fossils in limestone quarries and thought that the rock containing them must have been formed from soft sediments.

In the sixteenth century Leonardo da Vinci, always quick to trace cause and effect, studied fossils of sea animals and plants from limestone in the Italian hills. The original plants and animals, he decided, must have been buried in muds of a sea bottom. Somehow the muds turned to stone, which was then raised to become land.

But such ideas did not fit into the framework of human knowledge at that time. In 1800 even learned people still thought of Earth—with all its rocks—as created by one Divine Act. They could see that some kinds of rock consist of cooled lava from volcanoes. But as for rocks that obviously had formed in water, such as layered limestone and shale, these must be packed muds from Noah's Flood!

The 1800s were half gone before the origins of the main rock types were clearly distin-

guished. Scientific classification came only after long, careful observation by geologists out on the land, and with better techniques of chemical analysis.

THE ROCK FACTORY

Sedimentary rocks are more common on Earth's surface than any other rock type. They lie on the granite continental blocks like a patchwork quilt with holes here and there. Locally they may be found on valley bottoms, hillsides, mountain summits, or sea bottoms.

Formation of sedimentary rock begins with the accumulation of rock waste or other mineral materials on land or under water. The sediments may consist of erosion debris deposited on valley bottoms, plains, beaches, or sea bottoms. Or they may be bottom accumulations of mineral material from dead animals and plants and from chemical processes in the water.

The sediments build up, layer on layer, for thousands and millions of years. Lower layers

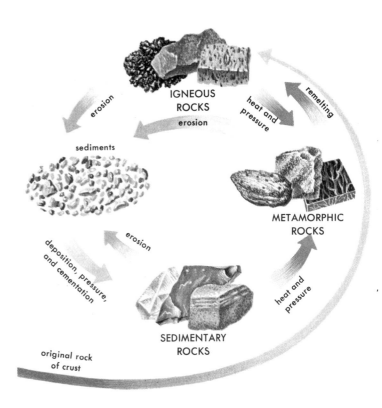

The rock cycle—*Sedimentary rocks form from mineral material deposited in water or deposited on land by wind. They may be converted into igneous or metamorphic rocks, or may disintegrate and be made into sedimentary rocks again.*

103

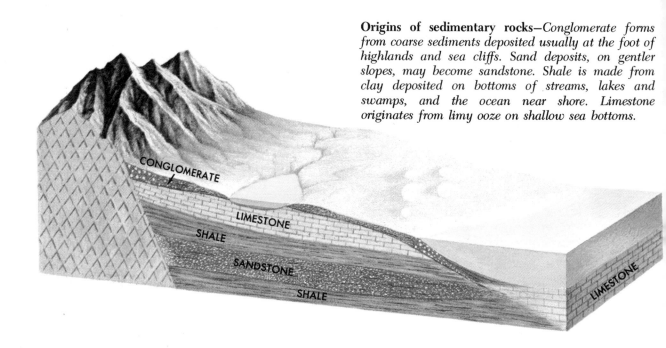

Origins of sedimentary rocks—*Conglomerate forms from coarse sediments deposited usually at the foot of highlands and sea cliffs. Sand deposits, on gentler slopes, may become sandstone. Shale is made from clay deposited on bottoms of streams, lakes and swamps, and the ocean near shore. Limestone originates from limy ooze on shallow sea bottoms.*

become packed hard by the increasing weight above and perhaps also by squeezing from earth movements. Particles become cemented together as water percolates down through them, depositing natural cements such as lime and silica. Thus over long periods the sediment becomes stone.

STONE FROM CLAY AND SAND

Shale, also called mudstone, is by far the most common of the sedimentary rocks, making up over 50 per cent of the entire group. Shale contains tiny clay particles, often produced by weathering and erosion of igneous rocks such as basalt and granite. Clay particles, smaller than sandstone grains, accumulate in quiet water because they settle slowly. They are found on delta edges, lake beds, and bottoms of bays and shallow seas.

Seen in cliffs, shale often appears as thin, crumbly sheets or flakes, but may be found also as thick, hard slabs. Colors range from red, brown, and green to blue, gray, and black.

Sandstone, which makes up about 20 per cent of sedimentary rocks, consists of grains larger than those in clay. The grains may be of many kinds, such as quartz, hornblende, and feldspar from granite or fragments of limestone, basalt, shale, and other rocks.

Most sand grains are just large enough to see without a magnifying glass. Under a glass many different kinds and colors may be distinguished. Sandstone masses are seen in red, pink, and brown, and gray to white.

Most sands were deposited on valley floors and along shores with varying currents. Some sandstones, like those of Zion National Park in Utah, are ancient dunes that turned to stone. In areas where sandstone is native it has been a favorite building stone because it occurs often in thick slabs or blocks which are easily cut.

MEDIUM-GRAINED SANDSTONE

RED SANDSTONE (cemented by iron oxide)

ARKOSE (showing feldspar grains)

Ripple Marks in Sandstone

"CRAB ORCHARD" SANDSTONE

Closely related to sandstone is conglomerate. This is essentially a sandstone that contains numerous pebbles and cobbles, often of quartz. Hence the rock may be called "pudding stone." The pebbles have commonly, but not always, been rounded by abrasion on a streambed or a beach.

Conglomerate typically forms from very coarse sediments deposited as alluvial cones or fans at the foot of highland ravines, or as masses of wave-worked material along beaches beneath eroding sea cliffs. A well-cemented conglomerate is likely to be very strong, forming ridges where—as in the Folded Appalachians—folds of sedimentary rock have been undergoing erosion for a long time.

LIMESTONE AND DOLOMITE

The fourth main type of sedimentary rock is limestone. Some varieties have formed from limy sediments in fresh water, but most are derived from sediments in clear, shallow, warm seas, away from the mouths of muddy rivers.

Limestones consist mostly of calcium carbonate (lime), occasionally mixed with clay minerals. The color is usually white or bluish gray, sometimes pink, and even black.

Certain limestones form from particles of carbonate precipitated—that is, dropped out of solution—in water. Precipitation may be due to warming of the water, evaporation, or purely chemical reactions. Other limestones consist of masses of shells or other limy remains of sea animals and plants, piled up on sea bottoms through ages.

An especially interesting kind of limestone formation is the reef, built up in warm or temperate seas by coral animals or lime-secreting plants. Such reefs are being built today in the southwest Pacific and the Caribbean. Ancient reefs have been discovered in such places as the Canadian Rockies and the Alps—regions once covered by the sea. The Guadalupe Mountains of New Mexico, which contain Carlsbad

Debris of mountains—*Conglomerate near Suffern, N.Y., consists of naturally cemented rock waste from erosion of the Appalachian Mountains.*

Caverns, were cut from a huge reef about 250 million years old.

Chalk masses are a kind of limestone built of the remains of one-celled animals, "foraminifera," too small to see without a microscope. The famous white cliffs of Dover, England, are of chalk. In Kansas, chalk in some places has been carved into scenic pillars; also

Mountains of dolomite—*Among the most scenic parts of the Alps are the Dolomites of northern Italy. Pinnacles show the influence of vertical joints.*

Remains of a delta—*Black shale near New Paltz, N.Y., is weak and flaky, as are many other shales.*

Formed on a sea bottom—*A limestone outcrop near Russellville, Ky., shows the work of ground water.*

it contains fossils of the mosasaur, a giant swimming reptile.

Many limestones, especially those containing much clay, tend to be soft and crumbly. Strong limestone, like that quarried in southern Indiana, is fine for buildings and monuments, but it tends to become weakened and pitted by acids in the air of modern cities.

Portland cement, used in concrete for buildings, highways, and bridges, is made by heating limestone and shale together in a kiln.

Closely related to limestone is dolomite. This consists mostly of a carbonate in which the element magnesium has replaced calcium.

Dolomite usually is grayish and less soluble than limestone.

Limestone dissolves in water that contains carbon dioxide. In a humid region, therefore, limestone tends to weather and erode away faster than most other rock types. Thus in the Appalachians we often find valleys in limestone and ridges on conglomerate, a more resistant rock. It is in limestone that the greatest caverns, like Mammoth Cave and Carlsbad Caverns, have been hollowed out.

STORIES IN ROCKS

Some sedimentary strata formed from sediments deposited on a slope; for example, the side of a sand dune or the front of a delta. Most sediments were deposited in horizontal layers, with the oldest layer normally at the bottom and the youngest at the top.

To a skilled geologist, each sedimentary layer tells a story about the conditions under which the sediments were laid down. A layer of sandstone over conglomerate, for example, may mean that a period of erosion and deposition by moderately swift streams followed a period when the streams were swifter—powerful enough to transport the large pieces of stone found in the conglomerate. A layer of limestone beneath shale may indicate that a sea bottom with limy

Common Types of Shale

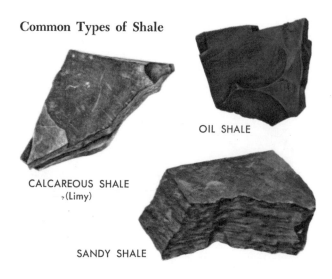

OIL SHALE

CALCAREOUS SHALE
(Limy)

SANDY SHALE

106

Plenty of chalk—*These deposits near Wind Cave, in South Dakota, consist mostly of remains of tiny sea organisms called foraminifers. Similar deposits are seen in Kansas and in England's famous Dover Cliffs.*

deposits was uplifted enough to become a coastal marsh where streams deposited mud.

Since the sedimentary layers are normally deposited in order, with the oldest at the bottom, they are like pages in a history book. By analyzing the layers in order, a geologist can tell how a region changed from age to age—for example, from sea bottom to delta to coastal plain to mountain range. Much of Earth's history has been reconstructed from clues in sedimentary rocks.

DEFORMED AND ALTERED STRATA

Sedimentary rocks do not always occur as neat, undisturbed layers. Often they have been warped, folded, or broken and moved out of position by crustal movements.

In some places magma has broken through sedimentary strata to form dikes, squeezed be-

Pages of a region's history—*Changes from stratum to stratum in sedimentary rocks are clues to changes in the environment during deposition.*

107

Mountains of sediments—*The Rocky Mountains originated with the folding and uplift of thick layers of sediments. Layering is apparent in these mountains in Jasper National Park, Canada.*

tween them to make sills, or arched them to build laccoliths. Sedimentary rock may become engulfed in magma and thus melt to become igneous rock.

Strata may be subjected also to metamorphism. Where mountains are being raised, deep-lying strata can be changed by heat, pressure, and infiltration by hot liquids and gases. Much metamorphic rock—slate, quartzite, and marble are examples—is made of materials that were once sediments.

PATCHWORKS AND SANDWICHES

More of Earth is covered by sedimentary rocks than by igneous or metamorphic rocks. Probably every part of the continents has at some time been blanketed by sediments.

Sedimentary strata that patch the continents were formed at different times and differ from place to place. Beneath the top stratum there are usually others, like slices of a many-decked sandwich. All have been to some extent warped, twisted, folded, or broken. Together they represent a sort of jigsaw puzzle of Earth history.

On most of western North America there are sedimentary rocks miles deep. Mostly they are covered by loose rock—"mantle"—and, especially in the Northwestern states, by deep lava flows. The northern Rocky Mountains expose limestones, shales, and sandstones that formed on sea bottoms. The central and southern Rockies were once covered with sedimentary strata, but these are now all but gone—stripped off by millions of years of erosion. At lower levels, from Montana to Arizona, are shales and sandstones deposited in rivers and lakes by streams and on dry areas by wind.

The Great Plains and the Mississippi drainage basin are on sedimentary rocks formed during periods when a shallow sea reached halfway into North America from the Gulf of Mexico. The marine sediments are covered by later accumulations deposited by streams, glaciers, and wind as the sea gradually withdrew.

Nearly horizontal sedimentary strata form the Appalachian Plateau, between the Mississippi Valley and the younger Appalachians to the east. The latter consist mostly of long folds trending southwest-northeast that began to form about 275 million years ago. Since then, uplift has kept pace as erosion has removed one to three miles of the sedimentary rock. The

108

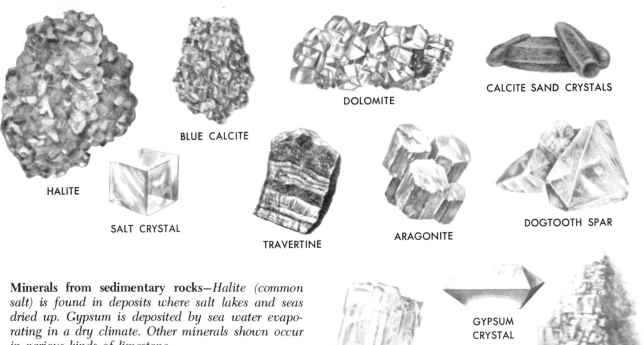

HALITE

BLUE CALCITE

SALT CRYSTAL

DOLOMITE

CALCITE SAND CRYSTALS

TRAVERTINE

ARAGONITE

DOGTOOTH SPAR

Minerals from sedimentary rocks—*Halite (common salt) is found in deposits where salt lakes and seas dried up. Gypsum is deposited by sea water evaporating in a dry climate. Other minerals shown occur in various kinds of limestone.*

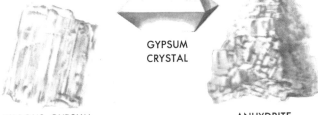

GYPSUM CRYSTAL

FIBROUS GYPSUM

ANHYDRITE

depth of the original sediments is estimated to have been as great as eight miles—their probable depth in North Carolina.

East of the younger Appalachians are older mountain groups, such as the Great Smokies, Hudson Highlands, Green Mountains, and White Mountains. All were formerly covered with strata that have been eroded off. Farther east, from the Middle Atlantic States south, are lowlands on red shale and sandstone.

Sculptures in sandstone—*Here at Colorado National Monument and elsewhere on the Colorado Plateau, erosion has carved horizontal sandstone layers into scenic blocks and pillars. Such scenery tends to be developed near plateau edges, where rainwater streams descend toward the lowlands swiftly.*

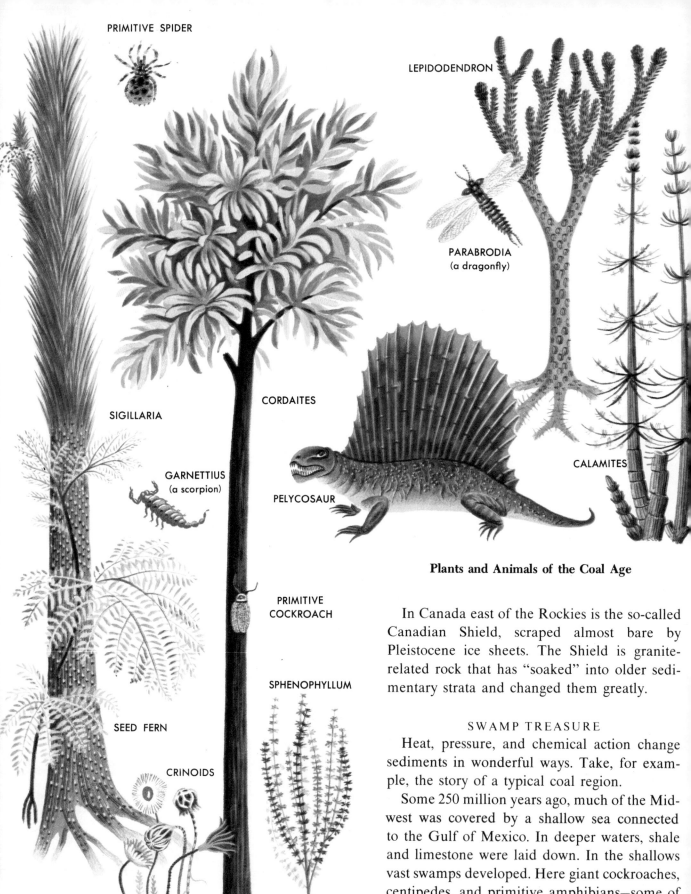

PRIMITIVE SPIDER

LEPIDODENDRON

PARABRODIA
(a dragonfly)

SIGILLARIA

CORDAITES

CALAMITES

GARNETTIUS
(a scorpion)

PELYCOSAUR

PRIMITIVE
COCKROACH

SPHENOPHYLLUM

SEED FERN

CRINOIDS

DIPLOVERTEBRON

Plants and Animals of the Coal Age

In Canada east of the Rockies is the so-called Canadian Shield, scraped almost bare by Pleistocene ice sheets. The Shield is granite-related rock that has "soaked" into older sedimentary strata and changed them greatly.

SWAMP TREASURE

Heat, pressure, and chemical action change sediments in wonderful ways. Take, for example, the story of a typical coal region.

Some 250 million years ago, much of the Midwest was covered by a shallow sea connected to the Gulf of Mexico. In deeper waters, shale and limestone were laid down. In the shallows vast swamps developed. Here giant cockroaches, centipedes, and primitive amphibians—some of the earliest land animals—crawled among masses of tall, fernlike plants. Overhead droned swarms of strange, clumsy insects.

The climate was warm and wet, and vegetation in the swamps was thick. Age after age the primitive plants pushed up through the black muck, grew tall, died, and crumpled down again. Age after age the dead plant material piled up.

Meanwhile the Appalachian uplift began. The swamplands began to rise, the sea gradually withdrew, and the swamps began to dry up. As the rising continued, erosion sediments from the highlands buried the old swamps to depths of thousands of feet. Finally, some 225 million years ago, the region had become a land of mountains and plateaus.

Buried deep in these highlands were layers of vegetation from the old swamps. Gigantic forces that had wrinkled the crust had squeezed the layers very hard. Where the material had been hundreds of feet deep it was now only yards thick.

Millions of years drifted by. The majestic Appalachians were slowly cut lower by erosion. As shales and sandstones blanketing the moun-

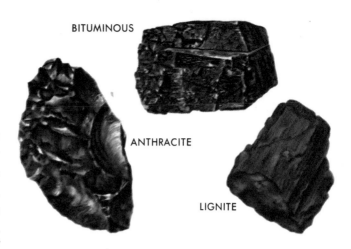

BITUMINOUS

ANTHRACITE

LIGNITE

The Three Principal Varieties of Coal

tains eroded away, parts of the old swamp layers began to show. They had become the black, rocklike substance we call coal—fuel and raw material for modern industrial civilization.

BLACK GOLD

Petroleum, too, is a treasure found in sedimentary rock. This liquid gives us gasoline,

"X-ray" of a coal mine—Shafts are driven down to coal seams, which are then tunneled. Shaft at left is for transporting miners; at right, for ventilation. At left a seam at the surface is being strip-mined.

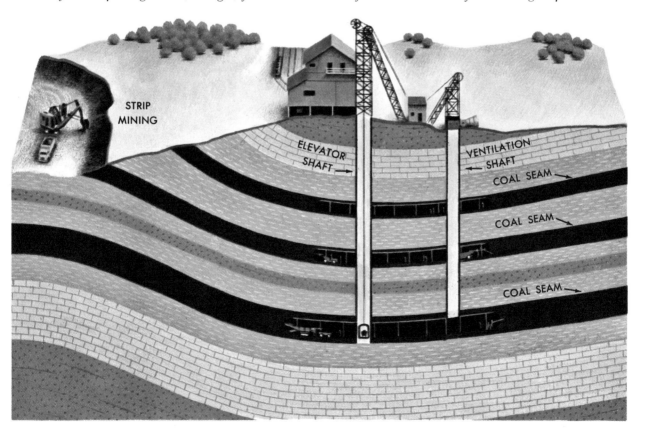

STRIP MINING

ELEVATOR SHAFT →

VENTILATION ← SHAFT

COAL SEAM →

COAL SEAM →

COAL SEAM →

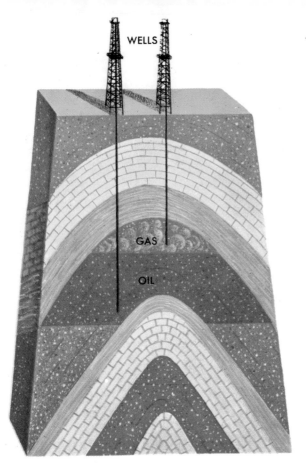

WELLS

GAS

OIL

Oil- and gas-producing strata—*Typically, oil and gas are trapped beneath rock folds called anticlines.*

heating and lubricating oils, and greases. From it are made a thousand and one other substances, ranging from plastics to artificial rubber and medicines.

Petroleum comes from remains of countless billions of plants and animals buried under water. As the sediments piled up and became rock, parts of the organic remains turned into oil and gas in tiny spaces between rock grains. Much of the gas and oil collected under arched rock strata ("anticlines") through which they could not escape to the surface.

Oil deposits have been found beneath the surfaces of all continents—under mountains and plains and lake beds, in polar regions and deserts, and in the sea-covered edges of the continental blocks. The largest known oil deposits lie beneath the deserts of Saudi Arabia.

Oil prospecting is done by drilling and by sounding—that is, blasting at the surface and studying the echo patterns that come back from rock strata below. The deepest oil well—in Texas—is more than five miles deep.

A limestone quarry—*At Tomkins Cove, N.Y., a 450-million-year-old deposit of limestone is blasted from cliffs and gathered by power shovels and trucks. Broken limestone is used in iron smelting. Ground-up limestone is used for soil treatment by farmers and gardeners.*

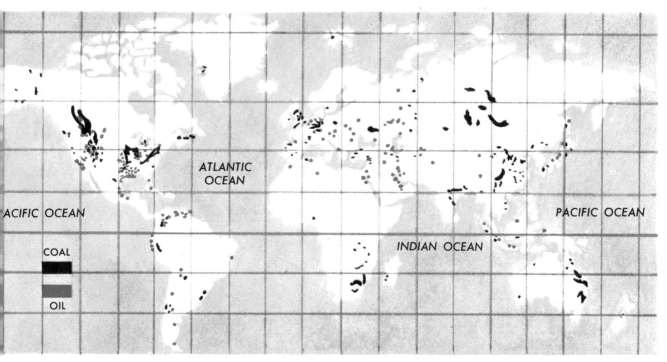

Oil- and Coal-producing Regions of the World

Industrial civilization has been using so much oil that most of it may be gone by the end of the twentieth century. Some oil can be obtained from coal, which is plentiful enough to last for several centuries. Oil can also be "cooked" out of oil shale—a rock consisting mainly of bits of dolomite with a waxy hydrocarbon, common in western Colorado and parts of Utah and Wyoming. Finding fuel for the future is one of the tasks of geology.

Is it promising?—*An oil-driller examines a sample of rock brought up by a core drill.*

Plants that became coal—*The plants were changed to carbon by heat and pressure, but their forms are preserved in remarkable detail.*

A rising coast—*The Pacific shore at Otter Crest, Oregon, displays a terrace cut long ago by wave action, then raised above sea level. Below is a new terrace. California's coast, too, shows such features.*

Lands Up, Down, and Sidewise

OLD EARTH seems as solid and stable as anything we know. Yet observant people since ancient times have realized that the land beneath us moves up, down, and sidewise.

There was the ancient Greek Anaximander, who wondered how it is that fossils of sea creatures exist in the rock of high mountains. And there was Leonardo da Vinci, who wondered about the same thing and decided some sea bottoms must have been raised to become dry land.

People living along seacoasts notice direct evidence of land movements. In Finland and Sweden, along shores of the Baltic Sea, farmers find seashells in fields hundreds of feet above sea level. Old residents have seen parts of the sea bottom rise to become islands.

Since ancient times, towns along Mediterranean shores have sunk underwater. Some scientific investigators think the Lost Continent of Atlantis, long considered a myth, was actually a Mediterranean land that sank during violent volcanic eruptions and earth movements in the fifteenth century B.C.

Earthquakes often bring clear signs of crustal movements. During the Alaska quake of 1964 part of Montague Island was raised 39 feet. During the San Francisco quake of 1906 fences were knocked as much as 21 feet out of line.

Geologists recognize less obvious signs of earth movements. Most mountains are known to result from uplift along with folding and faulting. Marine fossils in sedimentary rocks on continents show that the ocean has invaded lands that sank. Terraces on seacoasts such as those of Oregon and California are recognized as uplifted wave-cut benches. Valleys of rejuvenated streams also indicate uplift. Depressions

114

like Death Valley, California, are understood to result from sinking of crustal blocks. Warped, folded, broken, and dislocated rock strata betray earth movements. Finally, of course, there are changes in land elevation shown by surveyors' measurements—for example, the measurements that show the Baldwin Hills area of Los Angeles, California, to be rising approximately 2 to 3 feet per century.

During Earth history crustal movements have been the rule rather than the exception. No part of the crust is ever perfectly still.

LANDS UP AND DOWN—GENTLY

Most crustal movements are slight; they produce great changes only because they occur repeatedly over long periods. Thus the gradual sinking of the Chesapeake Bay region over millennia has allowed the ocean to creep scores of miles up its valleys. The Atlantic Coast from Maine to Connecticut has sunk slowly during the past few million years. The Salisbury Plain of southern England and the Paris Basin of western France are sea bottoms recently raised to become coastal plains. England's Cornwall coast and the northern shores of Scotland are, by contrast, sunken lands.

Gentle uplift is now going on where the Pleistocene ice sheets covered land and pressed it down. The ice melted thousands of years ago, but "crustal rebound" continues and will continue for thousands of years more. From Michigan to Maine rebound is occurring at rates up to 20 inches per century. In Canada's Hudson's Bay region, where glacier ice was miles deep, rebound since the ice melted, some 5,000 years ago, has been nearly 1,200 feet, and perhaps 1,000 feet more is expected. As much as 700 feet of rebound has occurred in Sweden and Norway. The British Isles, almost completely covered by Pleistocene ice, also are rebounding.

The invading sea—*Probably all parts of North America have been invaded by the ocean at some time during geologic history, then have risen to become dry land again. The upper map here shows maximum coverage of the continent by the sea in the Cambrian Period, 450 to 425 million years ago. The lower map shows coverage during Cretaceous time, 100 to 80 million years ago. Speckling indicates coastal-plain areas.*

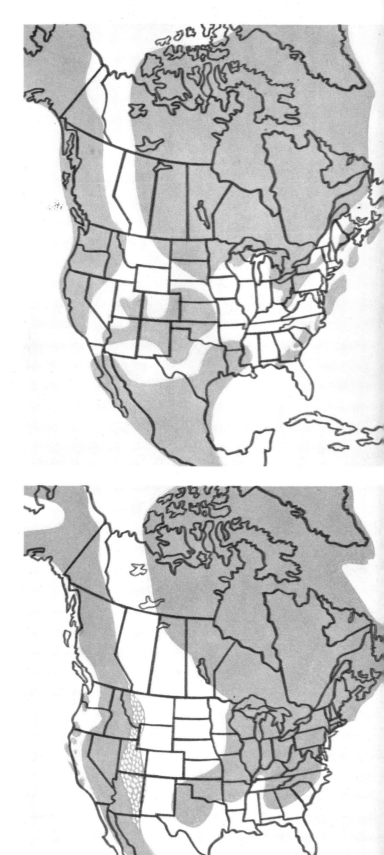

Appalachian folding—*A roadcut near Newfoundland, N.J., exposes a syncline and an anticline in sandstone. The folding occurred during the formation of the Younger Appalachians about 250 million years ago.*

Effects of earth movements may last long after movements have stopped—or reversed. The coast of Maine was sinking before the Pleistocene ice came; the seaward ends of its valleys were invaded by the ocean. Then the Pleistocene ice depressed the land further. Now the ice is gone and the coast is rising—but it still has the nature of a sunken coast.

THE STRANGE STORY OF FOLDING

Where parts of the crust are pushed hard and long against one another, folding is likely to occur, especially if the rock is layered. That, in fact, is how most mountain ranges are made. Folding that makes mountains can be compared to the rumpling of a tablecloth on a table when one side of the cloth is pushed toward the other.

Over millions of years, as earth forces act on rock, the rock grains move slightly to ease the stress or strain. Inside a fold, where the rock is being squeezed, grains move closer together. On the outside, where the rock tends to be pulled apart, spaces between the grains may open up a little or the rock may crack, or rock layers may slip over one another like pages of a paperback book when the book is bent. Over long time spans rock may fold like dough or taffy.

A monoclinal mountain—*Looming Mt. Timpanogos, in Utah's Wasatch Range, shows a great monocline in its broad limestone face.*

A common type of fold is the anticline. This is an upfold, or arch. Anticlines may be as big as mountains or as little as a thumbnail.

The opposite of an anticline is a syncline—a downfold, or upside-down arch. Synclines and anticlines often form in series.

Another kind of fold is the monocline. An example is a rock layer that runs horizontal, then bends upward, then levels out again.

Most folds are not symmetrical. They tend to lean one way or another; they may twist, or run straight and then curve. Almost any form is possible.

Many folds "plunge." They become shallower toward one end. Folds that become shallower toward both ends are said to be "doubly plunging."

Folds are features mainly of mountain regions. Small ones are seen in cliffs and in walls of quarries and roadcuts. Some folds are so large that only parts of them can be seen.

LANDSCAPES ON FOLDS

As folds rise to become highlands, streams on them speed up, and so does erosion. The folds are cut lower and lower. Because the rock layers differ in resistance, the land surface resulting from erosion tends to be uneven, as the diagram on the next page shows.

A synclinal mountain—*Canada's De Smet Range, in Jasper National Park, exhibits this broad syncline.*

Hogbacks—*These tilted sandstone strata are near Valyermo, Calif., along the San Andreas fault.*

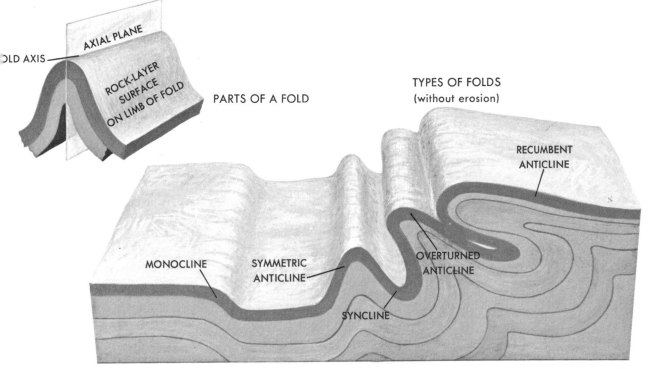

AXIAL PLANE

FOLD AXIS

ROCK-LAYER SURFACE ON LIMB OF FOLD

PARTS OF A FOLD

TYPES OF FOLDS (without erosion)

RECUMBENT ANTICLINE

MONOCLINE

SYMMETRIC ANTICLINE

OVERTURNED ANTICLINE

SYNCLINE

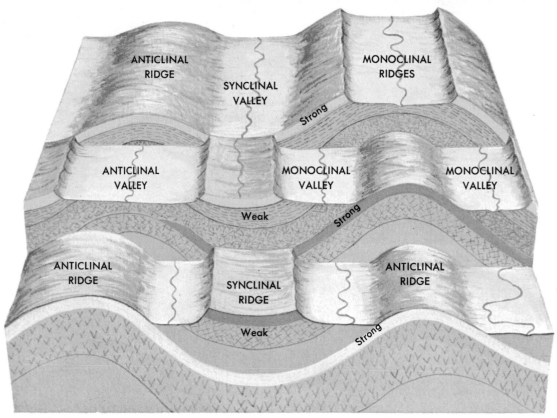

A landscape produced by erosion of folds—*Relatively strong rock, whether in an anticline, a syncline, or a monocline, tends to form highlands. Lowlands develop on weaker rock.*

One common landform on folds is the anticlinal ridge. Its cross section is an anticline. The ridge exists because the top layer of the anticline is relatively resistant. If erosion breaks through this layer into a weak layer beneath it, rapid erosion in the weak layer will make a valley lengthwise in the ridge. This will be an anticlinal valley.

Another common form is the synclinal valley, with a syncline as its cross section. Layers inside the syncline are relatively weak. If erosion removes these and reaches strong layers beneath them, erosion within the syncline will slow down and the syncline will become a synclinal ridge if the land on both sides is lowered more rapidly.

Types of faults—*Faults often occur along with folding. They are seen most commonly in cliffs and other such exposures in mountain regions. The patterns of rock dislocation may be very complex.*

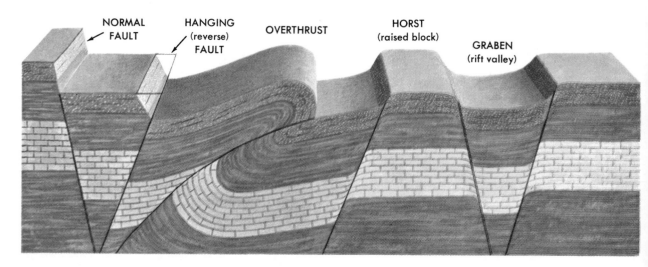

A vertical fault—*Here, in the Apache Mountains of Arizona, the sandstone mass at the left was raised or the mass at the right was lowered. Note the crushing of rock along the fault plane.*

As a fold is being cut into by erosion, the edges of steeply tilted layers that are relatively strong become ridges. Valleys form along the edges of weaker layers.

A ridge formed by the edge of a steeply tilted layer will probably be narrow and sharp-backed, with steep sides. Such ridges are known as hogbacks. A side of the ridge formed by edges of layers is a scarp slope. The side parallel to the plane of the layers is the dip slope.

Erosion on slightly tilted layers may produce a cuesta (KWES-tuh). This is a ridge with a long, nearly horizontal dip slope and a short, steep scarp slope.

The Folded (Younger) Appalachians, stretching from Nova Scotia to Georgia, are a "museum" of folds. These are best seen in roadcuts and cliffs nearly perpendicular to the axes (lengthwise directions) of the folds. The northern Rockies from Montana into Canada show fine folds in broad, bare cliffs. Many folds are visible in the Coast and Transverse Ranges of southern California.

Among the greatest exhibits of folding are the Alps of Europe. Here every imaginable kind of fold, and parts of folds, are seen in the towering mountain walls.

Among relatively old mountains, folds in sedimentary rocks are likely to be less noticeable. Usually the sedimentary layers have been eroded off and only mountain cores are seen. These consist mainly of granite and metamorphic rocks which were not folded or which have been so much altered that the folds are hard to discern. Examples of such mountains are the Great Smokies, the Hudson Highlands, and the New England mountains, and the Grampians of Scotland.

WHEN THE CRUST BREAKS

All bedrock shows fractures, or breaks, made by natural forces. Some are caused by tension, or pulling apart of the rock. This happens as igneous rock cools and contracts, or as any kind of rock is stretched by folding or twisting. Breaks may be due also to compression (squeezing) or shearing (cutting).

A fracture with no movement on either side is called a joint. All large rock masses are somewhat jointed. Joints may be short, thin, shallow

A fault scarp near Salina, Utah—*Note the row of triangular "facets," typical of the younger fault scarps. Facets result from narrowing of the small valleys toward the bottom. Narrowing is due to the fact that the scarp is younger toward the bottom and, therefore, the valleys are younger (and narrower) too.*

cracks at the surface or long, wide cracks hundreds of feet deep.

A fracture with movement of a rock mass parallel to the fracture surface is a fault. Movement may be vertical, horizontal, or oblique.

Vertical movement up or down makes a vertical fault. In a normal (gravity) fault the upper rock mass moves diagonally downward relative to the lower mass. In a reverse (thrust) fault the upper mass moves diagonally upward.

If, in this fault, the upper mass moves over the lower one at a very small angle over a distance of miles, the fault is called an overthrust. A normal or reverse fault that involves horizontal movement is a tear fault.

LANDSCAPES ON FAULTS

Faults produce or influence landforms. A highland called a horst results from rising of a crustal block. A depression called a graben

The graben of Death Valley, Calif.—*In this great depression is North America's lowest point—282 feet below sea level. This view is north from mouth of Desolation Canyon.*

Four geologic provinces—*The Rockies originated by folding, faulting, and uplifts. With these disturbances the Colorado Plateau area was uplifted, with little folding. The Great Basin is a wide, irregular depression with streams leading into it but not out. The Columbia Plateau was made by volcanic activity.*

is made by sinking of a block. A tilt block, the most common landform due to faulting, is produced by the tilting or tipping of a block so as to form a highland with a long backslope, sometimes extending down to a depression called a fault trough.

Ground areas on opposite sides of a tear fault are displaced, or offset, horizontally. The offsets may show as zigzags in a fence or highway, or as parts of a valley or ridge shifted sideward.

Landforms made by faulting are common where the crust has been active during recent geologic time. The Basin and Range Province (mainly Nevada, western Utah, southeastern California, southern Arizona, southern New Mexico) is a land of tilt blocks, grabens, and fault troughs. California's Sierra Nevada, with its east-facing fault scarp, and Utah's Wasatch Range, with its west-facing scarp, are the largest of the Basin and Range highlands made by tilting. California's Death Valley and Salton Basin (or Trough) are two of the largest Basin and Range grabens.

Wyoming's Teton Range, with an east-facing fault scarp, is formed by a tilt block. The Colorado Plateaus (western Colorado, southeastern Utah, northern Arizona, northeastern New Mexico) are a cluster of upwarped and uplifted blocks bounded partly by faults.

A Basin and Range tilt block—*Tilting of the sedimentary strata is apparent in the Peloncillo Mountains near Las Cruces, New Mexico. The profiles of tilt blocks often suggest that of a sinking ship.*

"**Garden of the Gods**"—*Here, near Colorado Springs, Colo., vertical sandstone strata of the Front Range have been eroded into a fantasy of fin-like hogbacks. These hogbacks are stumps of sedimentary strata that once covered the Rockies. Beyond the hogbacks here is Pikes Peak.*

The northern Rockies from Colorado into Canada show much overthrust faulting. Nearly everyone who has visited Glacier National Park, in Montana, has heard of the Lewis Overthrust. During the rise of the Rockies a huge slab slid east some 15 miles along a north-south line about 200 miles long. Chief Mountain, east of the park, is the remains of the slab; the rest has been destroyed by erosion. Overthrusting is indicated by the fact that the rock of Chief Mountain is older than the rock under it, reversing the normal order of rock layers. A transported block or slab like Chief Mountain, moved and cut off from its place of origin, is called a klippe (KLIP-uh).

Most faulting in rocks of the Eastern states occurred during periods of Appalachian activity earlier than 200 million years ago. The landforms produced directly by the faulting have been totally destroyed by erosion. The patterns, or relative arrangements, of highlands and lowlands today result from erosion of bedrocks

Evidence of earth movements—*Tilted sandstone strata at Vasquez Rocks, Antelope Valley, Calif., are examples of deformation in San Andreas fault zone.*

An ancient fault uncovered by erosion—*A scarp marks the course of the fault near MacDonald Lake, Canada. Uplift at the left was renewed in recent geologic time. During the Pleistocene this landscape was scoured by ice sheets.*

of varying resistance. The ancient faults, which reached deep into the earth, changed the relative positions of strong and weak rock masses, and thus have influenced the relative positions of the highlands and lowlands of today.

The most spectacular scenery in Europe is offered by the Alps. Raised mostly during the past 25 million years, they show folding and faulting so complicated as to drive geologists to despair. Among the striking features are huge recumbent folds (folds lying on their sides) and klippes—such as the Matterhorn—consisting of rock masses moved tens of miles during Alpine folding.

An interesting feature in Germany is the horst known as the Black Forest Plateau. West of it the Rhine River flows through a graben. The Vosges area in France is another horst.

Southern Europe, including the Mediterranean islands, has been much jumbled by recent faulting. Along the coasts, crustal blocks are sinking, carrying cities and towns with them. Many Mediterranean islands are horsts. The numerous klippes include the bold hill in Athens called the Acropolis, and also the rock masses that loom above the Straits of Gibraltar—the Rock of Gibraltar on the north and Jebel Musa on the south.

Severe earthquakes from the eastern Mediterranean region to India evidence continuing earth movements. Many highlands and lowlands result from relatively recent faulting. One is the graben that contains the Dead Sea and the Jordan River. The floor of this depression, nearly 400 miles long and 10 to 25 miles wide, is about 1,200 feet lower than the level of the Mediterranean Sea. Farther south is the long chain of depressions known as the African Rift Valley, extending from Syria to Northern Rhodesia in Africa.

From Sea Bottoms to the Clouds

EARTH'S history divides into ages of relative calm and shorter periods of unrest. Forces build up in the crust for a time and then break loose. For tens of millions of years there is much folding and faulting, uplift and subsidence, earthquakes and volcanic activity. Then, so it seems, the underground forces sleep again.

It is during times of unrest that new mountain ranges are born. They originate in various ways. Some are built up by lava as cones or shields. Others are masses of igneous rock formed at depth, then uplifted and uncovered by erosion. Many mountains are formed by the tilting or raising of crustal blocks. Among the most impressive mountains are those of the fold type.

FOLDS INTO MOUNTAINS

The creation of a fold mountain range begins with a sea-filled hollow usually at least 1,000 miles long and scores or hundreds of miles wide, called a geosyncline. This crustal trough gradually fills with sediments from erosion and sea water, and its bottom sinks lower and lower. Through ages the sediments become miles deep.

After millions of years, opposing forces in the crust begin to squeeze the sedimentary rock layers, folding and breaking them. Magma from depth surges up through fractures, melting some of the layered rock and bursting out from the crust to form volcanoes. Meanwhile the trough bottom rises and the sea withdraws.

Gradually the folds rise as mountains, their roots mixed with igneous rocks deep in the

High world—*Mountains, Earth's noblest scenery, are raised by slow spasms of the crust. This view is from Middle Needle near Mt. Blanc, French Alps.*

**Biography of the Appalachian Region
(spanning 500 million years)**

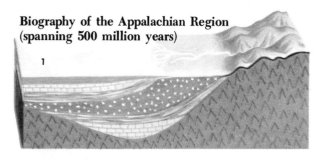

Sediments are laid down in a geosyncline, forming shale, limestone, and sandstone strata. The bottom of the trough sinks as the weight increases.

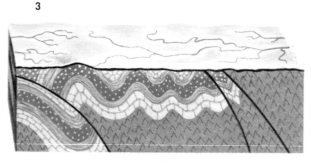

The land rises, the sea retires, and the strata are folded, faulted, and uplifted to make mountains. As uplift proceeds, streams erode the land.

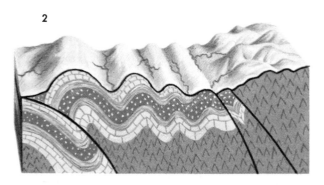

Gradually erosion cuts off the tops of the folds, reducing the region almost to a plain. The streams lose gradient and their ability to erode.

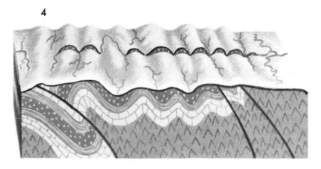

New uplift of the region rejuvenates the streams, starting a new erosion cycle. The Appalachians have seen six or seven such cycles completed.

earth. As they heave up, sedimentary rocks along their edges may rise, without folding, to form plateaus, in which rock layers are nearly horizontal. Among or near the mountains, volcanic eruptions may build cones or spread lava widely to make plateaus of basalt. Magma may cool in the crust to make sills, dikes, and larger igneous masses—laccoliths, stocks, batholiths. Crustal blocks near fold mountains may rise, sink, or tilt to make highlands and grabens.

The basic cause of mountain-building is movements of the plates that make up the planet's crust. The nature of these movements, and the story of how geologists have come to understand them, are the subject of a later chapter.

MOUNTAINS DOWN

As mountains rise, erosion grinds them vigorously. Valleys are cut in zones of weaker rock, ridges on stronger rock. Over long ages the land is sculptured into shapes that show the nature and arrangements of the rock layers.

The building of a range may take 25 million years. But the rate of building up is faster than the rate of eroding down. The mountains may reach heights of four to six miles. Then uplift slows and erosion takes over. The mountains are ground lower and lower, eventually perhaps becoming a rolling peneplain—that is, a land reduced nearly to a plain by erosion.

THE APPALACHIAN STORY

Nearly a billion years ago, the ocean bottom off eastern North America (which looked very different at that time) was a geosyncline loaded with sediments miles deep. Rearing up from the bottom were a chain of active volcanoes like those of the Hawaiian and Aleutian Islands today. In time the sediments, turning to rock, were folded and lifted to become a land mass with peaks up to 10,000 or 15,000 feet.

Millions of years went by. Uplift waned; the mountains were eroded low. West of the mountain stumps a new geosyncline developed, as much as 500 miles wide and several thousand long. Through ages sediments collected here to depths of 8 miles. Then began, about 250 million years ago, a new phase of mountain building. Earth forces thrusting northwestward squeezed the sedimentary layers into long folds, some twisting or zigzagging, several miles high.

Meanwhile the stumps of the old mountains to the east were subjected to new folding and faulting, and were raised several thousand feet.

As uplift slowed, about 200 million years ago, erosion became dominant. But faulting continued, with tilting of crustal blocks. Volcanoes along the edges of the mountains spewed lava over the land. Magma cooling between sedimentary layers formed dikes and sills—including the Hudson Palisades sill.

During more millions of years the highland landscape was worn down to a low, rolling plain. Then it was lifted a few thousand feet again, and still again erosion speeded up. There have been perhaps a half dozen such cycles.

Such is the story—much simplified—of the Appalachian Mountains. The Older Appalachians (those that date back nearly a billion years) include Maine's Katahdin and other highlands, parts of the Green Mountains and Berkshire Hills of Vermont and Massachusetts, the Adirondacks and Hudson Highlands of New York, and the Blue Ridge and Great Smokies of Virginia, North Carolina, and Tennessee. The Younger ("Folded") Appalachians are the long ridges that include the Shawangunks and Bellvale Mountain in New York and Bearfort and Kittatinny Mountains in New Jersey, then extend diagonally down through central Pennsylvania, over the western parts of Maryland and Virginia, through West Virginia and into eastern Tennessee, and finally die out in northern Alabama.

West of the Folded Appalachians is the Appalachian Plateau, with nearly horizontal rock layers. Swift streams cutting into higher parts of the plateau near its eastern edge have made many deep, narrow valleys, separated by high ridges. These deeply sliced lands are known as the Catskill, Pocono, and Allegheny mountains —though not, strictly speaking, true mountains.

The Appalachians of today look different from the originals. Erosion has all but destroyed once-proud peaks and spread the debris over the Atlantic Coastal Plain and sea bottoms. In the Folded Appalachians only stumps of great rock folds remain. The Older Appalachians are essentially uplifted and uncovered mountain roots—masses of sedimentary and igneous rock metamorphosed to schist, gneiss, quartzite, and marble.

Today the Appalachians are relatively quiet; erosion rules. In time these mountains may be ground down to sea level--or raised again.

MOUNTAINS TO THE WEST

The history of the Rocky Mountains is more complicated. The present Rockies, from the northwest corner of Canada down into New Mexico, rise from a very old part of North America, dating back two billion years and

Stumps of an ancient range—*The Great Smokies are among America's oldest mountains. The view is of Newfound Gap near the Tennessee-North Carolina boundary.*

Conglomerate hogbacks in the Rockies—*These slabs, in the Front Range near Boulder, Colo., are stumps of sedimentary strata that originally arched across the Rockies.*

more. The earliest mountains were eroded away long ago, but parts of their roots remain—deformed, faulted, much-altered rocks. The region's long history involves several cycles of mountain-building and volcanic activity, erosion, and new invasions by the sea.

The Rockies of our age date back to an ancient seaway extending from the Arctic Ocean to the Gulf of Mexico. Beginning some 60 or 70 million years ago, miles-deep layers of sediments in the trough were folded, faulted, and uplifted as mountains several miles high. During the next 25 million years these were peneplained. Then, about 25 million years ago, uplift started again and the eroded mountain stumps rose up to be carved into fine new peaks. Meanwhile, in areas nearby, crustal blocks tilted and volcanoes poured out lava to make additional highlands. Recent erosion, particularly glaciation, has sculptured and worn the rejuvenated Rockies, but they still rise to heights of nearly three miles.

Diversified is the word for the Rockies. In western Canada and Montana they are mainly of sedimentary layers, in the east strongly folded and thrust-faulted, and in the west uplifted with less folding. The Colorado Rockies are mostly granite and metamorphic cores of ranges that originally arose as broad-backed folds, from which the sedimentary layers were then eroded off, leaving scenic hogback stumps along the mountain margins. In southern Colorado are the San Juan Mountains, an enormous heap of eroded lava beds. Wyoming has the Absaroka Mountains, similar to the San Juans, and the Teton Range, the upper part of a tilted fault block. New Mexico's Sangre de Cristo Mountains are a jumble of fold, volcanic, and tilt-block highlands. Volcanic and block mountains are scattered over Nevada, New Mexico, Arizona, and west Texas.

The newest Western fold mountains are the Coast and Transverse ranges of southern California. These are now being pushed up, with much folding and faulting, to the tune of earthquakes. The cause is the northward glancing thrust of the Pacific Plate against the North American Plate.

A "CHAOS" OF ROCK

About 200 million years ago, a gigantic geosyncline stretched from southwestern Europe to southeastern Asia. In it was the Tethys Sea, ancestor of the modern Mediterranean. During the past 70 million years this geosyncline has produced a vast array of mountains, including —to name a few—the Pyrenees of France, the Atlas of Africa, the Pindus of Greece, the Carpathians of eastern Europe, the Caucasus east of the Black Sea, the Himalayas of northern India and Nepal, and—not least—the Alps.

For geologists the Alps are jigsaw rock puzzles. Developed mostly during the past 25 million years, they show all varieties of folds— open and closed, rounded and pointed, narrow and wide, twisted and broken, lying down, upright and tilted and upside down, and—in places—broken and dragged tens of miles from their places of origin.

During the Pleistocene, the Alps had tremendous snowfalls because of their nearness to the Mediterranean, and they were strongly sculptured by valley glaciers. Their valleys, already deep from intense folding, were cut even deeper by the ice. Earthquakes near the mountains indicate that unrest continues today. Recent uplift has not kept pace with erosion, but the region is still impressive, with looming cliffs, icy peaks, and sweeping valleys.

Geologists have spent lifetimes trying to determine from jumbled strata what happened in the Alps. These mountains have been compared—with some exaggeration—to slices of a marble cake tossed randomly into a heap.

BLOCKS INTO MOUNTAINS

Mountains produced by the raising or tilting of crustal blocks may be associated with fold mountains. The numerous block mountains of North America's Great Basin are mostly far from the Rockies but were raised at about the same time and are undoubtedly related.

An entire mountain range—such as the Tetons —may be formed by a single tilt block. A gentle backslope and a steep fault scarp are typical.

Tilt blocks are more common than horsts. Usually a tilt block is divided by lesser faults.

Scrambled rock in the Alps—*The diagrams approximately indicate the evolution (bottom to top) of the Alps in the Jura region. The geosyncline phase (1) is followed by uplift with folding and thrust faulting (2 and 3) and the final carving of the mountains by the Pleistocene glaciation.*

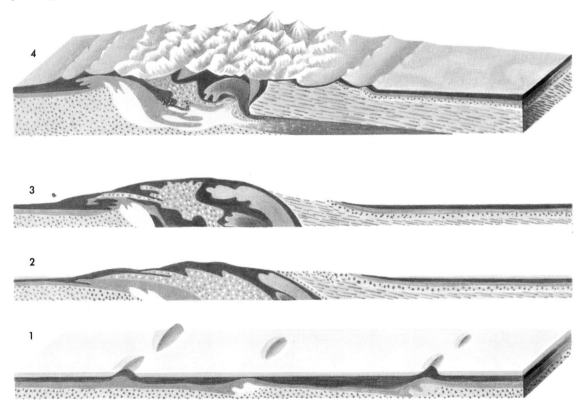

Edge of a giant tilt block—*The Sierra Nevada of California and Nevada have been shaped on a long, up-raised block with an east-facing fault scarp. Part of the scarp is shown here.*

Faulting may mix up strong and weak rock masses, so that as the mountains are eroded they often acquire a jumbled look compared to the Younger Appalachians, with their relatively regular folds, and the Colorado Rockies, with their often smooth granite profiles. The jumbled look of many block mountains is especially apparent in the desert, where weathering and erosion are inadequate to round off the rock masses, and where mountain profiles may not be gentled by a cover of trees.

Blocks tilted within the past few million years are common in the northern and western parts of the Great Basin—Nevada, Utah, southern California. The fault scarps are not yet destroyed by erosion; they still have facets—that is, triangular surfaces which are remnants of the surface originally exposed by faulting (see page 120). In southern Arizona and New Mexico tilting occurred earlier, for the most part, so that the original fault scarps have been eroded away.

One great tilt block of the Great Basin area is the Wasatch of Utah. Its west-facing scarp, 130 miles long, rises about 4,000 feet above

Great Salt Lake. The scarp still shows facets.

Much larger is the Sierra Nevada tilt block of California and Nevada. Tilted about 20 million years ago, it consists of uplifted granite roots of fold mountains dating back some 150 million years. The present range extends about 400 miles north to south and is as much as 75 miles wide. The east-facing, faceted scarp rises nearly 10,000 feet above the Owens Valley in the Great Basin. The long western back-slope, covered with sedimentary rocks, plunges beneath the Pacific.

In northwestern Wyoming rises the Teton tilt block, about 60 miles long north to south and some 20 miles wide. Its east-facing fault scarp rises more than a mile above Jackson Hole, a graben to the east. The tilting began about 50 million years ago; after long erosion there was another uplift. Today erosion is king again, and the glorious peaks are wasting away.

MOUNTAINS OF LAVA

Volcanic mountains develop along deep crustal fractures. Build-up of lava on ocean floors

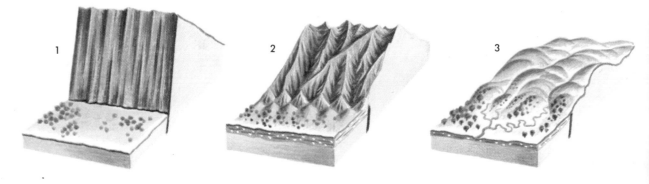

Erosion of a tilt block—*At left (1) is the tilted block as it would look without erosion. Next (2) is the block while erosion is shaping it during uplift. Finally (3) the worn-down block is shown as it might appear long after uplift ceased and after many millions of years of erosion.*

to make undersea mountains is thought to have been the first step in the creation of the continents. Today the process continues in Central America and Mexico, the Aleutians, Hawaii, the Philippines, Indonesia, Iceland.

Most of today's estimated 500 active volcanoes are in the "ring of fire" around the Pacific Ocean (see map, page 134). Additional volcanoes cluster in the northern Atlantic, along the Mediterranean, and down the east side of Africa. Large volcanic ranges rise from seafloors.

Active volcanoes deep within the continents are rare. But extinct cones can be recognized in many interior sections. From California to Colorado, and from Washington to western Texas and Arizona, we find cones that were active within the past 20 million years. Farther east, volcanic activity dates back to the remote past, and the cones have all been eroded away. However, geologists recognize volcanic necks and plugs in New Jersey and Virginia. Parts of the Older Appalachians consist of volcanic rocks nearly a billion years old. Volcanic mountains have probably existed in most parts of the world at one time or another.

FROZEN RESERVOIRS

Some of our greatest mountain scenery has been carved from batholiths—reservoirs of granite formed miles deep, then uplifted and uncovered by erosion. Batholiths tend to rise gradually, perhaps because the granite is a little lighter than surrounding rock. Since granite is more resistant than most other rock types, erosion tends to leave a batholith standing as a highland after uncovering it.

The Black Hills of South Dakota have been carved from a batholith about 125 miles long and 65 wide. Granite peaks rise 4,000 feet above surrounding lowlands of sedimentary rock.

The Idaho Batholith, exposed over 16,000 square miles, has been sculptured to make the Clearwater, Salmon, Sawtooth, and Coeur D'Alene mountains.

The continent's greatest granite reservoir is Canada's Coast Range Batholith. This forms the Coast Mountains, spanning 1,000 miles from British Columbia to the Yukon.

Mountains sculptured from "stocks"—frozen reservoirs of magma that fed volcanoes—are found in several Western states. Among them are Utah's Henry, La Sal, and Abajo mountains and Navajo Mountain. In southern Colorado are the Spanish Peaks and the San Miguel and La Plata mountains. Stocks in western Montana include parts of the Crazy Mountains and Judith Mountains. Around some stocks are laccoliths forming lesser peaks.

A mountain range made of lava—*Oahu, like the other islands of Hawaii, was built miles high from the Pacific's bottom by volcanic outbursts of the past million years. The range seen here is Koolau.*

Lisbon, Portugal, on Nov. 1, 1755—*The great earthquake collapsed buildings, started raging fires, and produced a tsunami that overwhelmed the city and took 10,000 lives.*

When Earth Trembles

DEEP in Earth are gigantic forces that build mountains and move continents.

In most parts of the world people have little reason to think about these forces. But in other regions there are sudden and terrible reminders. The underground forces build up like steam pressure in a boiler. For months, years, even centuries, they build up. Then all at once some weak part of the crust reaches its limit of endurance and breaks. The sudden release of pent-up energy shakes the crust violently. This motion, like the vibration of a released bowstring, is an earthquake.

At the surface a quake may be announced by underground rumblings and reports like distant artillery fire. Then the ground starts moving. The motion may be up and down or side to side—usually both. If the earth material beneath the surface is moist sand or clay, lying over the bedrock, it may shake like jelly.

Earthquakes can make boulders dance, shake trees out of the ground, knock down people, flatten buildings. Long, ragged cracks may appear in the ground, and on opposite sides of a crack the ground may slide in different directions for several yards, twisting buildings out of shape and putting curves in fences, highways, and railroad tracks. It all may happen in a minute or two—or may continue on and off for weeks.

Ordinary well-constructed buildings can stand a few jolts or slow back-and-forth movements. But the motions are sometimes unbelievably rapid. Buildings are literally shaken to pieces. People are killed or injured by falling roofs and walls. Fires start from cooking stoves, lamps, and broken electrical wiring. Faults break water mains, so that there is no water available for fighting the spreading fires.

Earthquakes may trigger landslides. Whole

villages have been buried by cascades of rock shaken loose from steep slopes.

Underground forces may be so finely balanced that a thunderstorm or a wind can set off a quake. And one quake may start others.

TOKYO: 1923

One of the worst of all recorded earthquakes was the one that hit the Japanese cities of Yokohama and Tokyo a half century ago. These cities lie near the shores of Sagami Bay. On September 1, 1923, the bottom of the bay suddenly sank and the whole region shook with shattering force.

A shipmaster out in the bay, who happened to be looking toward Yokohama, saw its buildings bobbing up and down like small boats on rough water. The city was all but leveled.

Tokyo was not shaken so hard, but fires broke out there, as in Yokohama, and water mains parted. Before the disaster was over all of Yokohama was a smoking ruin and half of Tokyo was flat. The damage came to several billion dollars, and 140,000 people died among fires and falling buildings.

SAN FRANCISCO: 1906

In the United States the worst earthquake was the one that shook San Francisco in 1906. At five in the morning, when most of the city was still asleep, the tremors began. People on the streets staggered and fell down. Walls dropped out of the sides of buildings. Water mains broke and flooded the streets. Fires starting in buildings could not be checked in the panic. The city burned for days and about 450 people lost their lives.

The San Francisco quake resulted from a sudden movement of the crust along the San Andreas Fault. Land on opposite sides of the fracture shifted as much as 21 feet.

MOUNT HUASCARAN: 1970

In Peru on May 31, 1970, occurred an earthquake of the kind that triggers a disastrous landslide. Severe tremors centered near Chimbote, lasting a mere 45 seconds, leveled a group of towns in Huaylas Valley, killing 16,000 of a population of 65,000. The disturbance loosened a half-mile-wide slab of rock and ice on the north side of nearby Mt. Huascarán, a 22,205-foot volcano—the highest mountain in Peru. Down roared the crumbling slab, lubricated by mud and melting ice beneath it, and riding a cushion of trapped air. At an estimated speed of 275 miles per hour, 35 million cubic feet of rock and ice swept down the valley, grinding to bits everything in its path. Within two minutes scores of villages were gone and 50,000 more people were dead. The worst landslide in recorded history was over.

TSUNAMI: "TIDAL WAVES"

A faulting movement beneath a sea bottom suddenly lifts or drops a large volume of water. A wave runs outward at a speed of 400 to 500 miles per hour. It may be only a foot or two high but is 100 to 400 miles long and thus contains far more water than ordinary wind-made waves. The low height of the wave allows it to pass unnoticed under a ship at sea, unless the ship has special detection equipment. When

What causes an earthquake—*(1) Rock strata in the crust, subjected to uneven pressure or tension, start to crack. (2) The force of deformation increases. (3) Finally the crust breaks with a great shivering or shaking—an earthquake.*

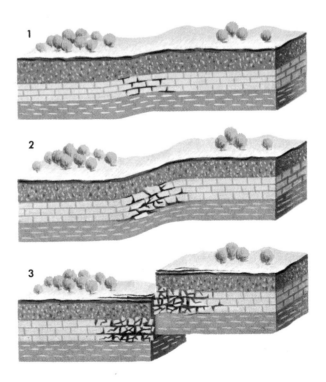

Regions of unrest—*The yellow areas are where earthquakes are most frequent or most severe. These areas tend to be regions of volcanic activity (shown by red dots) and mountain building.*

the enormous volume of water reaches land, it builds up as a giant breaker with devastating possibilities.

A great wave of this kind is known as a tsunami (tsoo-NAH-mee)—the Japanese word for "storm wave." The term "tidal wave" also is

"Drunken" houses—*The San Francisco quake of 1906 shook houses off their foundations, left them reeling.*

used—inaccurately, because the wave is not caused by the forces that make a tide (mainly the gravitational attractions of Moon and Sun).

Destruction by tsunami has been extensive on islands of the western Pacific, including Japan and Indonesia. When Krakatoa Volcano blew up in 1883, water rushed into the great hole made by the explosion. This movement raised a wave 75 to 100 feet high which swept over Java and Sumatra, drowning 30,000 people.

During an earthquake centered near Lisbon, Portugal, in 1755, a 50-foot wave leveled the lower part of the city. In 1960 a series of earthquakes and tsunamis along the coast of Chile caused millions of dollars' worth of damage and the deaths of several thousand people.

A tsunami can travel thousands of miles. Those that started near the coast of Peru during the big quake of 1877 traveled 10,000 miles, reaching Japan in about 21 hours. They were 8 feet high at the end of their journey.

Fortunately there is advance warning when a tsunami is about to come in. Just as water along a beach withdraws before an ordinary breaker comes in, so the water withdraws before a tsunami arrives. But in this case the amount of water withdrawing is far greater.

It is as if the tide went from high to low in a minute or two. Then in comes the towering—and perhaps devastating—wave.

THE PERENNIAL TERROR

In ancient times, earthquakes even more than volcanic eruptions were events of terror. Quakes were always unexpected and usually extremely destructive. Violent shaking of a town meant collapsing stone buildings, fires sweeping wood or thatch dwellings, flooding of streets by river or sea water, and panicked people trampling one another as they fled. Accounts of quakes are common in legends of people in the Mediterranean region—an area subject to many quakes during our geologic era.

Earthquakes were little understood by philosophers of old, who attributed them to fires, winds, or waters raging underground—or simply to the wrath of gods. Our modern understanding comes from long scientific study of the crust, including world-wide use of an instrument called the seismograph.

AN ALERT WATCHMAN

The seismograph, ingenious yet simple, is built on the pendulum principle. The frame is anchored in bedrock. One end of the pendulum is attached to the frame, and the other end, which is quite heavy, is left free. When an earthquake shakes the bedrock, the frame shakes with it. The free end of the pendulum has a slower, different motion.

Also anchored in the bedrock is a rotating spool of photographic paper. Upon the paper falls a steady beam of light coming from the free end of the pendulum. As the spool unrolls, the beam "draws" a continuous line on the moving paper.

During a quake the bedrock vibrates. So does the spool. But the beam of light, coming from the pendulum, has its slower, different motion. Thus the line it makes on the paper is wavy, and so the earthquake is recorded. The more severe the earthquake, the bigger are the waves on the line.

The seismograph is very sensitive. The line drawn is always slightly wavy, showing that slight movements continually occur in bedrock. When a strong quake occurs anywhere in the world, seismographs placed at various stations record it.

The epicenter of a quake—that is, the location on the crust where the shocks are strongest—can be determined by analysis of the shock waves. These include different types. Primary (P) waves are compression waves, traveling through bedrock like sound waves through air. Secondary (S) waves move like loops along a rope shaken at one end. P-waves travel at 5

Earthquake souvenirs—*The quake of August 15, 1959, in Montana's Hebgen Lake region disrupted Route 287 and made a 5-mile-long, 180-foot-deep lake where the Madison River was blocked by a 90-million-ton landslide.*

Pressure (P) Waves
during three successive instants

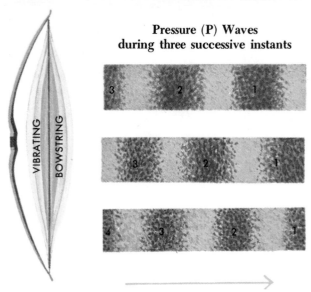

P-waves suggest vibration of a bowstring (left) but travel as diagrammed here (at right).

Transverse (S) Waves

S-waves suggest loops in rope shaken at one end. Diagram shows traveling loops at successive moments.

miles per second, S waves at 3. When a quake occurs, P waves reach the seismograph first. The distance from the epicenter to the seismograph is proportional to the time lag of the S-waves behind the P-waves.

Seismograph stations are maintained in many countries by government agencies and universities. Recording is continuous. When strong tremors are detected, the stations check with one another to determine the location of the epicenter (see diagram). Sometimes a severe

Seismograph principle—*Difference between vibrations of spool (anchored in bedrock) and pendulum (hanging on spring) is recorded as zigzags of line on spool.*

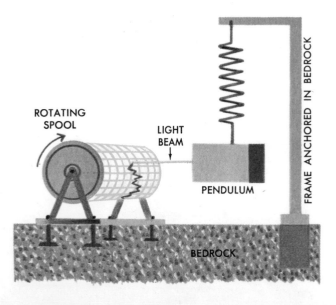

quake and its exact location are announced to the world days before the news arrives from the stricken region.

Seismographs reveal an average of several thousand earthquakes per day. Most are so slight that only the seismograph can detect them. About 25 quakes per year do serious damage to life and property.

Most quakes start along faults in the crust not deeper than about 40 miles. Some occur at depths up to 100 miles, and a very few at depths of 400 miles or so. The significance of major quakes at depth is told in later pages of this book.

The strength of an earthquake is rated scientifically on the Richter scale. A rating of 2 is

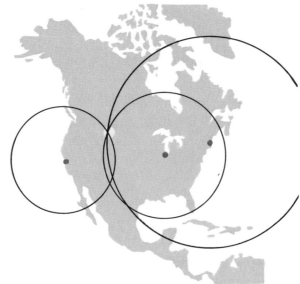

Locating an earthquake—*Distance of epicenter from each of three stations is determined. With this distance as radius, a circle is drawn around each station. Epicenter is about where circles meet.*

ten times as strong as a rating of 1; a rating of 3 is ten times 2; and so on. A 2.5 quake can barely be felt by a person. A rating of 7.0 or more indicates a major disturbance.

Southern California's earthquake of February 1971, which took 62 lives, was rated 6.6. The Peru quake of 1970, which triggered the catastrophic avalanche, was rated 7.9. The Alaskan quake of 1964, which did $500 million in damage and killed 131 people, rated 8.5. Casualties in the Alaskan quake would have been far worse but for the fact that the quake was centered in a sparsely populated area.

EXPLORING BY SEISMOGRAPH

Seismic waves do not report disasters only. They yield data from which scientists learn about Earth's interior.

Seismic waves, like sound waves, pass through different kinds of bedrock—basalt and shale, for example—at different speeds. Also, they are refracted (changed in direction) as they pass at an angle from one rock mass into another. Thus waves from a quake will travel at unequal speeds and along crooked paths while passing through different bedrock masses. When they reach seismographs at various locations, their times of arrival, directions, and other characteristics will be a clue to the rock types and structures through which they have traveled. By means of these clues scientists can explore the planet's interior from either land surfaces or sea bottoms.

Seismographs are widely used in prospecting. In an area where masses of valuable minerals are thought to exist below the surface, small explosions are set off at various places. Seismographs placed nearby record these explosions. Data obtained indicate the kinds of rock strata

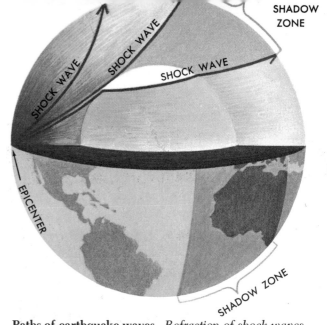

Paths of earthquake waves—*Refraction of shock waves traveling through Earth gives clues to structure of planet's interior. Shadow zone is area where, because of refraction, shocks are not noticed.*

below, their order and thickness, their tilt, and locations of pockets or layers where minerals are likely to be found.

EARTHQUAKE PROPHETS

Throughout history man has tried to predict earthquakes and control them by magic or

Oil prospecting—*Blasts are set off at the shot points, creating seismic waves. These are reflected differently from rock strata of different types. Detectors record the reflected waves. Analysis of the waves indicated the relative positions of the strata and the likely locations of oil.*

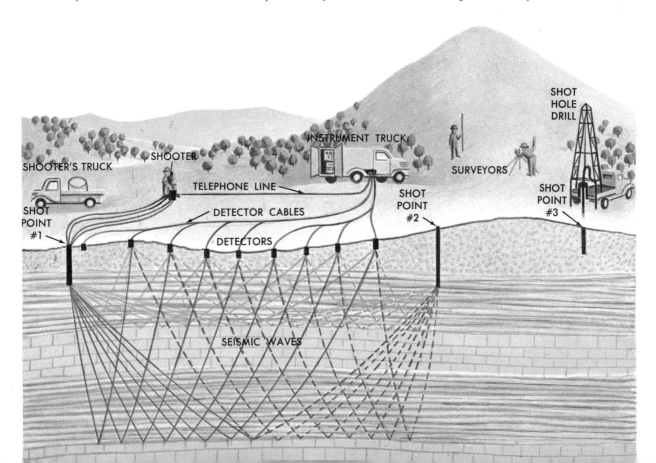

prayer. Even in the age of science, prediction remains uncertain and efforts at control have been in vain.

Quakes are most likely to occur in active fault zones where quakes have occurred recently. In active volcanic regions quakes may precede, accompany, or follow eruptions. Major tremors may occur with a kind of rhythm—for example, about every 60 years along the San Andreas Fault.

Changes in the crust give some hints of coming quakes. The ground may tilt, for example, or magnetic patterns in the crust may change because of increasing stress or strain. There is some evidence, not yet entirely reliable, that changes in the ratio of P-wave speeds to S-wave speeds from a certain region indicate an imminent disturbance there.

Some scientists believe small tremors would release crustal forces before these build to dangerous proportions. They recommend that explosions be set off in earthquake-prone areas from time to time. But other scientists fear that small tremors might trigger big ones.

Many quakes are like those along the San Andreas Fault, where a crustal block on one side of the fault is scraping against the block on the other side. The blocks tend to catch, hold for a while, then break loose, causing a quake. It has been suggested that water could be forced into the fault under high pressure to "lubricate" it and prevent the catching. This idea arose some years ago when injection of water from a nuclear plant into the ground near Denver, Colorado, produced minor tremors. Such ideas hold hope for the future.

Scientists are following all leads in their effort to learn how to predict and, some day, control earthquakes. Meanwhile they strongly recommend laws to improve the design of buildings, bridges, power lines, and other structures in earthquake-prone areas. They also urge adequate planning to meet earthquake emergencies—which are sure to come, sooner or later.

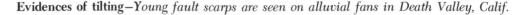

Evidences of tilting—*Young fault scarps are seen on alluvial fans in Death Valley, Calif.*

Metamorphic rock—*Contorted mica schist is common in the region of Mt. Mansfield, Vermont.*

The Changed Rocks

OUR planet's interior, from zone to zone, is always active. Crustal forces squeeze, bend, and stretch the bedrocks. Magma boils up from the mantle. Mineral-bearing water and gases percolate through joints and between rock grains. It is no wonder that rock masses change in shape, texture, color, and chemical composition. Such are the changes—called "metamorphism"—that produce the metamorphic rocks.

A PUZZLE SOLVED

Metamorphic rocks have long been a scientific problem—or set of problems. They are known to form, without melting, from igneous and sedimentary rocks. But the ways in which the rocks change are not precisely or completely understood. If these rocks perplex modern geologists, we can understand why the Neptunists and Plutonists were confused about them. The Neptunists called them "sedimentary"; the Plutonists, "igneous."

James Hutton was excited to find sedimentary strata strongly folded and compressed, and apparently changed chemically. He wondered. A half century later Lyell, traveling widely and putting together his picture of Earth's past, realized that metamorphic rocks must be old rocks transformed by heat, pressure, and the filtering of various chemicals through them. Still later the Canadian geologist Sir William Logan

showed that the "foundation" of North America is a mass of metamorphic rocks and granite.

ROCK FACTORIES DEEP DOWN

Sedimentary and igneous rocks thousands of feet down in the crust are under great pressure, especially during mountain building. Such pressures squeeze round pebbles in conglomerate into the shapes of eggs or jelly beans. Under super-pressures little pockets of carbon can become diamonds. Pressure can make molecules of hard rock rearrange themselves to occupy less space.

Rocks at depth are "cooked" by heat from pressure or invading magma. Minerals change chemically, becoming minerals of other kinds. Gases and liquids in magma filter into surrounding rock, moving between the molecules, reacting with them to produce still more changes in mineral composition.

Ground water can percolate thousands of feet down into the crust. On the way it dissolves small amounts of mineral, such as quartz or calcium carbonate, from rock through which it passes. It may deposit this material in rock lower down. These deposits act as natural cements between rock grains. Pressure may then cause rock and cement to crystallize together.

Such are typical processes by which metamorphic rocks are created. These rocks, as al-

ready suggested, are commonly found in regions of mountain building—that is, regions of great crustal pressures and of fracturing that allows magma to surge up from depth. Formed miles down, metamorphic rocks may later be exposed at the surface by erosion and faulting.

QUARTZITE: CEMENTED SANDSTONE

When water is poured onto a heap of dry sand, it sinks in rapidly. There is plenty of space for the water between the sand grains.

Sandstone also has spaces between the grains. Ground water percolates down through them, depositing mineral between the grains. If the deposits are of quartz, if the sandstone is made mostly of quartz grains, and if pressure is sufficient, a new kind of rock is formed: quartzite.

Quartzite fractures into blocks, often fairly rectangular. Surfaces on fresh breaks have a sugary look, because the breaks occur through the quartz grains, not around them (as happens with ordinary sedimentary rock). Because quartzite is so hard and chemically very stable, it is one of the most resistant of all common rocks. When exposed by erosion, it tends to stand above weaker rocks, forming highlands.

SLATE: BLACKBOARD ROCK

Who hasn't written with chalk on a blackboard? Until recently, blackboards in schools were choice sheets of the metamorphic rock slate. Today this is used more for flagstones.

Slate comes from shale. With a microscope one can see in it the interlocking crystals of quartz, mica, and clay. In some pieces of slate one sees bands which are the edges of layers of the original shale. The slate may break parallel to these layers or across them.

In resistance to weathering and erosion, slate is higher than most other rocks. Being sheety and brittle, it is not much used as building stone, but it does make durable roofing material.

HORNFELS: COOKED ROCK

Clay or shale "cooked" at depth, but not melted, may metamorphose into hornfels. This is a dark, often somewhat sheety rock that still shows the original sedimentary layers. Hornfels can be looked for along the margins of dikes and sills intruded into shale or clay. It may resemble basaltic rocks.

Quartzite outcrop in southern Vermont—_This exposure shows the typical blocky character of quartzite masses. Most quartzite is pinkish to gray-white._

GRAY SLATE

RED SLATE

PHYLLITE: "SILVERED" ROCK

Slate subjected to continued metamorphism may gradually become phyllite. This is a flaky, sheety rock, often with a silvery luster. As with slate, the sheets or flakes may or may not parallel the layering of the original shale. In a cliff one may see slate grading into phyllite through intermediate stages, or perhaps phyllite grading into schist.

SCHIST: CRINKLY ROCK

Among the most interesting of the metamorphics is schist (SHIST), derived from shales and igneous rocks. A pocket magnifier clearly shows interlocking grains of mica, hornblende, and quartz. Most schists are sheety or flaky, and the edges of the sheets may show very complex, crinkly folding. Mica schists have a high proportion of mica, the flakes of which are very shiny. Some schists form from phyllites and may grade into them. A strong schist may be cut for building stone.

THE GNEISS FAMILY

Among the most resistant of the metamorphics are those called gneiss (NICE). These generally come from impure sandstone and igneous rocks. The minerals are mostly feldspar, often with quartz, mica, and hornblende. The crystals may segregate to make layers, each of which contains mostly one kind of mineral. Many gneisses weather into big blocks. Gneisses are generally very resistant to erosion and thus, after becoming exposed at the surface, often make highlands.

MARBLE: LUXURY STONE

Probably the most valued of common rocks is marble, formed by metamorphism of limestone or dolomite. Marble is naturally white but may be tinted green, pink, black, or other colors by impurities. In some marbles fossils are found, though metamorphism tends to destroy them. Marble can be hard and strong but is soluble (as is limestone), so that in a long-eroded landscape marble is seen more in valleys than on ridges. Strong marble, not too closely jointed, is favored for fine buildings and monuments.

WANDERING MOLECULES

Where magma pushes between rock masses to make batholiths, dikes, and other igneous rock bodies, hot fluids penetrate between grains and molecules of the "host" rock. In this way impure sandstone, for example, can be converted through various stages into a gneiss. Many geologists believe granite, long considered to be completely of igneous origin, has in some instances been created in this way.

Possibly some granites have been created from sandstone and shale without the presence of any magma. In California's Sierra Nevada, a huge mass of granite is completely surrounded by sedimentary rock. There is no evidence that the granite was emplaced, or intruded, as magma. Nor are there any signs that the granite got

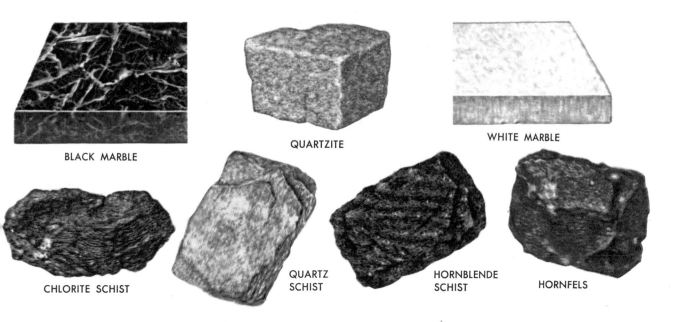

Metamorphic assortment—*Here are just a few of the many kinds of rocks produced by heat, pressure, and infiltration.*

BLACK MARBLE

QUARTZITE

WHITE MARBLE

CHLORITE SCHIST

QUARTZ SCHIST

HORNBLENDE SCHIST

HORNFELS

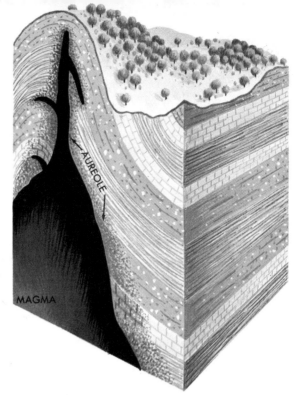

Left: **"Rock of ages"**—*This quarry has been blasted 350 feet down into Vermont granite—possibly an ancient metamorphosed sedimentary rock.*

there by dislocations due to faulting. Could it be that, over tens of millions of years, some of the sedimentary rock was changed to granite by the wandering and rearrangement of its own molecules? Such are some of the tantalizing questions faced by geologists today.

FOUNDATIONS OF THE CONTINENTS

Metamorphic rock, with granite, forms important parts of the continent "foundations." Continents probably began with the build-up of volcanic mountains along ocean-floor fissures. As the mountains eroded, the sediments collected in geosynclines. They were then folded and uplifted to become land. The upper parts were worn away, and the stumps buried beneath the sediments. Thus were formed the foundations on which continents were built by ages of volcanism, erosion and deposition, transformation of sediments into rock, and uplift.

The oldest parts of the continents consist of metamorphic rocks invaded by granite and mixed with it. Each continent has a core of such rocks, mostly covered with igneous, sedi-

Zone of change—*Where magma invades, surrounding "host" rock is metamorphosed to an "aureole."*

mentary, and metamorphic rocks that are younger (see map).

Radioactive dates of the foundation rocks go back three billion years and more. The oldest known rock is metamorphic—the Greenland gneiss mentioned earlier.

The continental shields—*Masses of metamorphic rock, with granite, apparently form the cores of the continents. The "platforms" are parts of shields covered mostly by sedimentary strata.*

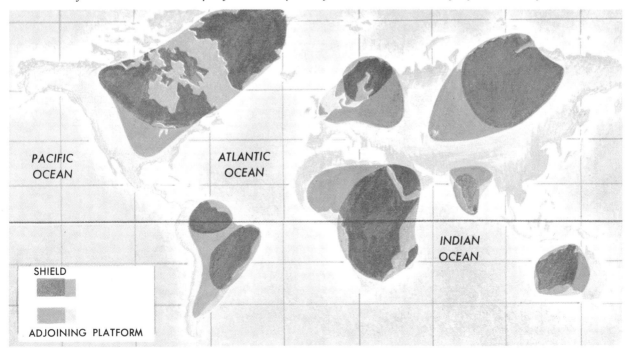

PACIFIC OCEAN

ATLANTIC OCEAN

INDIAN OCEAN

SHIELD

ADJOINING PLATFORM

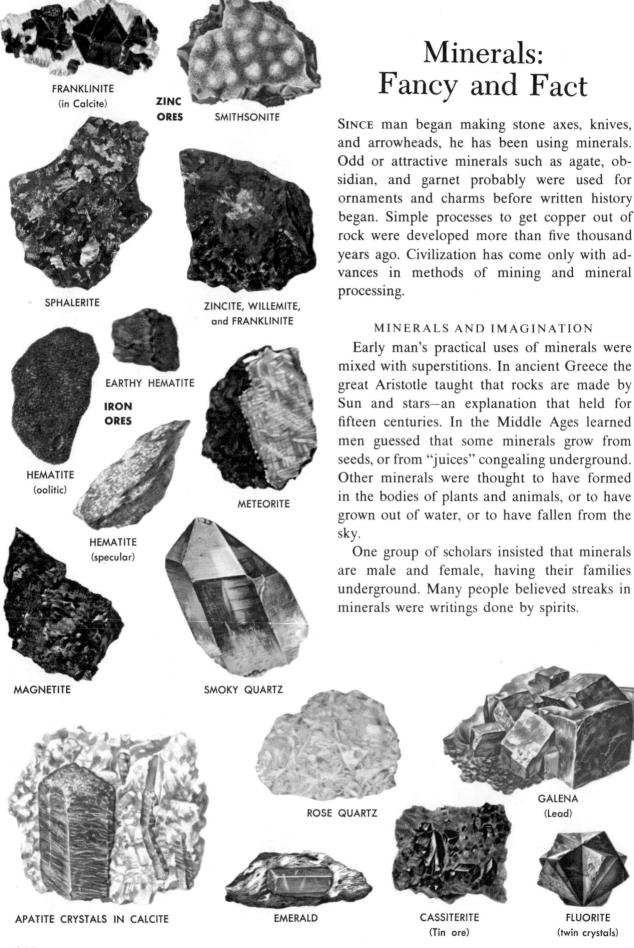

Minerals:
Fancy and Fact

SINCE man began making stone axes, knives, and arrowheads, he has been using minerals. Odd or attractive minerals such as agate, obsidian, and garnet probably were used for ornaments and charms before written history began. Simple processes to get copper out of rock were developed more than five thousand years ago. Civilization has come only with advances in methods of mining and mineral processing.

MINERALS AND IMAGINATION

Early man's practical uses of minerals were mixed with superstitions. In ancient Greece the great Aristotle taught that rocks are made by Sun and stars—an explanation that held for fifteen centuries. In the Middle Ages learned men guessed that some minerals grow from seeds, or from "juices" congealing underground. Other minerals were thought to have formed in the bodies of plants and animals, or to have grown out of water, or to have fallen from the sky.

One group of scholars insisted that minerals are male and female, having their families underground. Many people believed streaks in minerals were writings done by spirits.

FRANKLINITE
(in Calcite)

ZINC ORES

SMITHSONITE

SPHALERITE

ZINCITE, WILLEMITE, and FRANKLINITE

EARTHY HEMATITE

IRON ORES

HEMATITE
(oolitic)

METEORITE

HEMATITE
(specular)

MAGNETITE

SMOKY QUARTZ

APATITE CRYSTALS IN CALCITE

ROSE QUARTZ

EMERALD

CASSITERITE
(Tin ore)

GALENA
(Lead)

FLUORITE
(twin crystals)

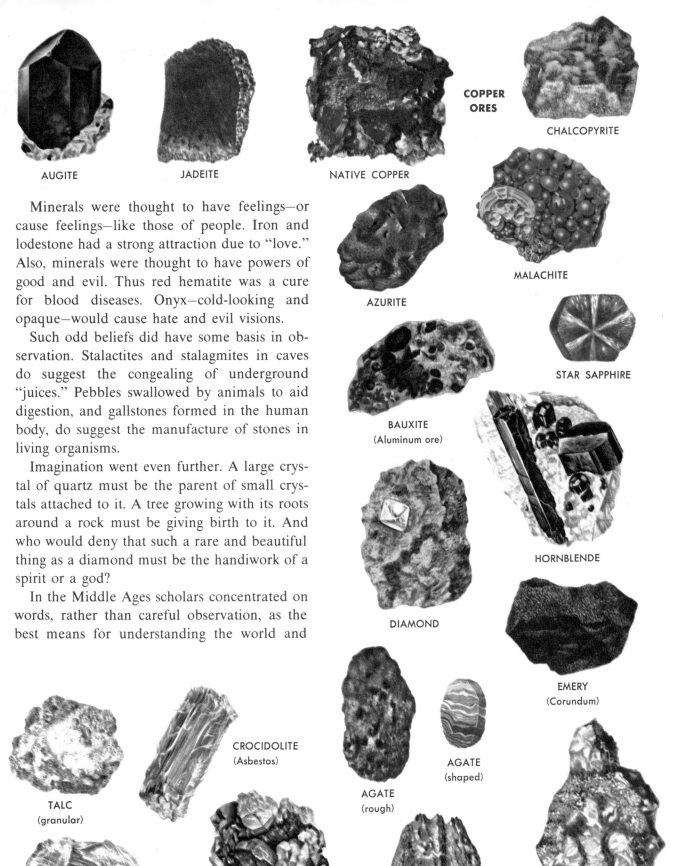

AUGITE

JADEITE

NATIVE COPPER

COPPER ORES

CHALCOPYRITE

AZURITE

MALACHITE

STAR SAPPHIRE

BAUXITE
(Aluminum ore)

HORNBLENDE

DIAMOND

EMERY
(Corundum)

TALC
(granular)

CROCIDOLITE
(Asbestos)

AGATE
(rough)

AGATE
(shaped)

TALC
(foliated)

ARGENTITE
(Silver ore)

GOLD ORE

GOLD
(in Quartz
with Pyrite)

Minerals were thought to have feelings—or cause feelings—like those of people. Iron and lodestone had a strong attraction due to "love." Also, minerals were thought to have powers of good and evil. Thus red hematite was a cure for blood diseases. Onyx—cold-looking and opaque—would cause hate and evil visions.

Such odd beliefs did have some basis in observation. Stalactites and stalagmites in caves do suggest the congealing of underground "juices." Pebbles swallowed by animals to aid digestion, and gallstones formed in the human body, do suggest the manufacture of stones in living organisms.

Imagination went even further. A large crystal of quartz must be the parent of small crystals attached to it. A tree growing with its roots around a rock must be giving birth to it. And who would deny that such a rare and beautiful thing as a diamond must be the handiwork of a spirit or a god?

In the Middle Ages scholars concentrated on words, rather than careful observation, as the best means for understanding the world and

MICROCLINE
(Feldspar)

LABRADORITE
(Feldspar)

SULFUR

SERPENTINE

ANORTHITE
(Feldspar)

ANORTHITE
(Feldspar)

ALBITE
(Feldspar)

RUBY

SKUTTERUDITE
(Cobalt ore)

ORTHOCLASE
(Feldspar)

MUSCOVITE
(Mica)

BIOTITE
(Mica)

COBALTITE
(Cobalt ore)

GRAPHITE

solving problems. They gave little attention to the natural properties of things. They left such matters to God, who had made everything. Experiments were left to alchemists— dirty, secretive men puttering around their crucibles with the dream of transforming lead into gold.

Even to us the real nature of minerals is not always obvious. Consider that common salt is made from a yellowish gas (chlorine) and a silvery-looking metal (sodium). Consider that lampblack and diamonds consist of the same element: carbon. No wonder people a few centuries ago, believing in magic and having little understanding of the chemical nature of the world, told themselves strange things about rocks and minerals.

A NEW LOOK AT MINERALS

Minerals began to be regarded as natural materials in the sixteenth century—a time when men were eagerly exploring the seas and the heavens, the air and the earth beneath.

Among the first with the new viewpoint was a German named Georg Bauer, better known as Agricola. (Most scholars then took Latin names and wrote in Latin.) He was a mining expert in Saxony, where flourishing industries were making the most of rich mineral deposits. Busy at getting ores out of the ground and processing them quickly and cheaply, Agricola had to brush aside useless superstitions and build up a store of practical information. His book *De Re Metallica*, published in 1556, classified minerals not as to magical properties but in ways that could help in identifying them, mining them, making them useful. He wrote of color and weight, transparency and luster, taste and odor, shape and texture—all good scientific terms. He noticed typical forms, such as those of quartz crystals, as well as hardness, combustibility, brittleness, and cleavage. He spoke

146

with scorn of those who wrote learnedly of magical properties.

Agricola grouped the kinds of rocks in which useful minerals are likely to be found. He grouped minerals according to their outward forms. Some of his classifications sound odd now, but they show his determination to see things as they really are. He is justly called the father of mineralogy.

The German mineralogist Abraham Gottlob Werner, leader of the Neptunists, followed Agricola's classifications generally but paid more attention to crystal forms and chemical makeup. The Frenchman René-Just Haüy founded the science of crystallography toward the close of the eighteenth century. A little later the Swedish chemist Jons Jacob Berzelius worked out chemical methods for mineral analysis. Today scientists use the principles of atomic physics.

WHAT MINERALS ARE

Minerals are combinations of chemical elements. The elements are made of atoms. The atoms consist of combinations of electric particles so tiny that there are billions in a pinhead.

In all there are over 100 chemical elements, many quite rare. In combinations the elements make up 1,500 to 2,000 kinds of minerals—the exact number depending on how precisely they are distinguished.

Most kinds of minerals are combinations of just a few elements. Thus ice consists simply of the gases hydrogen and oxygen. Quartz is made of silicon and oxygen. Calcite, the major substance in limestone, combines the metal calcium with carbon and oxygen. Carnotite contains the metals uranium, potassium, and vanadium, plus oxygen and hydrogen.

MINERALS FROM MAGMA

The richest mineral sources are rocks formed from magma or subjected to heat and infiltration by fluids from magma. Most mines are in mountain areas where magma has risen through fractures and strong metamorphism has occurred.

Metallurgy in 16th-century Germany—*This illustration in Agricola's* De Re Metallica *indicates that processing of ores was highly developed despite the lack of theoretical knowledge.*

As magma nears the surface, pressure on it lessens. The hot fluid begins to expand and cool. Some of it turns to gas; some solidifies. Thus minerals form.

No one has ever seen magma. But laboratory tests indicate how chemical substances act under great heat and pressure. Thus mineralogists know the probable order in which minerals form in a cooling magma or lava. Minerals with a relatively high melting point are among the first to form. Minerals with low melting points are generally among the last.

Magmas differ widely in the kinds of minerals and rocks they produce. The magma that is erupted as lava from Mauna Loa yields basaltic rock. The magma that feeds Mt. Vesuvius produces a rhyolitic, or granitic, rock.

Most rock originating from flow lavas and magma cooling underground consists of mineral crystals. The slower the cooling, the more time there is for the crystals to grow in size. Thus igneous rock formed at depth has larger crystals than igneous rock formed aboveground.

At depth, crystals can grow to the size of a house. But crystals in lava may be so small that a microscope is needed to see them. Rhyolitic lava can cool so fast that no crystals at all are formed. What results is the glassy and amorphous rock called obsidian.

Magma causes changes in host rock—that is, the rock it invades. Such changing is called contact metamorphism. When magma flows against sandstone, for example, large crystals of quartz may form in that rock. Heat from magma can produce crystals of garnet and mica in shale. A rich variety of minerals may be created when magma invades a limestone full of impurities, as happened at Franklin, N.J., one of the world's best-known mineral sites.

MINERALS FROM WATER

Some minerals are produced by the direct action of water. Ground water percolating through limestone, for example, dissolves out calcium carbonate and then may redeposit this as calcite crystals—the "travertine" of limestone

Open-pit mining—*This is a copper mine in Chile. Here, as elsewhere, the excavation is made with a spiral road around the inside for ore trains and trucks.*

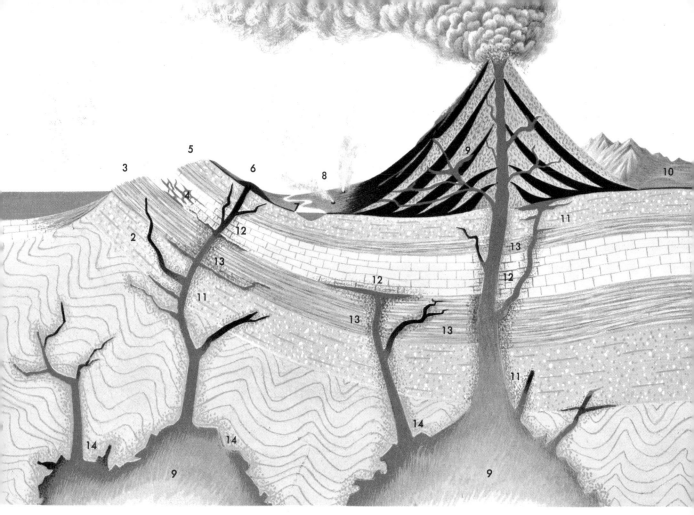

1 *Sea bottom:* calcite. 2 *Ore vein:* galena, sphalerite, chalcopyrite, pyrite, arsenopyrite, etc. 3 *Weathered shale:* kaolin, bauxite, other clay minerals. 4 *Limestone caves:* calcite, dolomite, gypsum. 5 *Weathered sandstone:* quartz. 6 *Weathered ore vein:* azurite, malachite, cuprite, anglesite, smithsonite, chrysocolla, cerussite. 7 *River valley:* placer deposits (gold, platinum, diamond, cassiterite, magnetite, ilmenite, garnet, zircon, monazite, rutile). 8 *Fumarole, geyser, and hot spring:* sulfur, hematite, geyserite, gypsum, opal, zeolites. 9 *Igneous rocks:* feldspars, quartz, olivine, pyroxene, hornblende, magnetite, biotite. 10 *Desert playa:* evaporation salts (common salt, potassium and magnesium salts, gypsum, borates). 11 *Metamorphosed sandstone:* quartz, feldspar, mica. 12 *Metamorphosed limestone:* calcite, dolomite, wollastonite, tremolite, diopside. 13 *Metamorphosed shale:* garnet, mica, quartz, feldspar. 14 *Contact zone:* garnet, epidote, pyroxene, hornblende, sulfides.

caverns. Streams running over the land dissolve salt and carry it to lakes or the sea. There it is deposited as the water evaporates. Some such deposits are now the sites of salt mines, as in New York state and Kansas.

Another mineral deposited on lake and sea bottoms is gypsum, or calcium sulfate. The marvelous dunes at White Sands National Monument near Alamogordo, New Mexico, are of gypsum particles. They were deposited by mountain streams in a Pleistocene lake, which dried up thousands of years ago.

In recent years rock samples have been dredged up from sea bottoms all over the globe. These samples are rich in manganese, cobalt, copper, nickel, and other metals that are becoming scarce. Of especial interest are the potato-sized manganese nodules.

Formed by reactions between lava and cold sea water, the metals are most abundant along the volcanic midocean ridges. They probably can be mined at depths of 2 to 4 miles by means of scraper buckets and devices like vacuum cleaners lowered from barges. How to divide up ocean-bottom mineral rights is already a major international problem.

MINERALS FROM THE SKY

Earth in its orbit keeps colliding with meteorites—fragments of hard material drifting in space. In passing through our atmosphere most meteorites heat up, partly melt, and vaporize

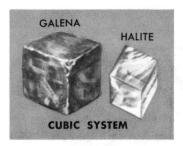

GALENA
HALITE
CUBIC SYSTEM

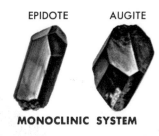

EPIDOTE   AUGITE
MONOCLINIC SYSTEM

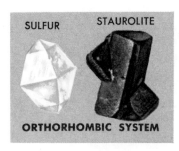

SULFUR   STAUROLITE
ORTHORHOMBIC SYSTEM

AMAZONSTONE   RHODONITE
TRICLINIC SYSTEM

ZIRCON   RUTILE
TETRAGONAL SYSTEM

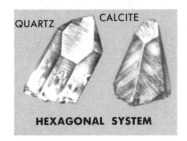

QUARTZ   CALCITE
HEXAGONAL SYSTEM

or disintegrate, but a few bits reach the ground. Every 500 years or so a big meteorite weighing hundreds of tons blasts a huge hole in the ground, such as Meteor Crater in Arizona.

Freshly fallen, unweathered meteorites have a smooth surface, due to melting. Some are mainly of iron and nickel, occasionally with cobalt. Others are stony, made of silicates.

Meteorites probably are fragments of a disintegrated planet or satellite. The Allende meteorite, the oldest so far tested, contains calcium-aluminum silicate with a radioactive age of 4.61 billion years—indicating that the solar system is at least this old.

Probably not more than a dozen specimen-sized meteorites reach the ground daily. Most meteorites weather away or become buried. Few collectors have the good luck to find one.

Another "sky" mineral is the tektite—a glassy (silicate) stone ranging up to the size of a walnut, often shaped like a teardrop or dumbbell, varying from jet black to yellow or olive green. Tektites are limited to a half dozen regions of the world (including the Caribbean area and southeastern United States), where they were strewn at different times during the geologic past. Some scientists believe they are bits of Moon rock melted and thrown out into space by meteorite impacts, then captured by Earth's gravity. But in chemical composition they differ from Moon rocks brought back by the Apollo astronauts. Tektites may, then, result from meteorite impacts on Earth.

MINERAL CHARACTERISTICS

Minerals come in all colors of the rainbow. One kind may turn up in different places with different colors. Quartz, for example, appears in white, rose, and other hues. Rose quartz gets its color from a tiny amount of iron oxide in it.

Each mineral has a certain way of cracking and splitting. Some split into flat sheets, as mica does. Some, such as calcite, break into neat blocks. Flint and many other minerals break like glass, leaving curved surfaces. Magnetite is one of many that show a grainy surface where they break.

The way each mineral reflects light—that is, its luster—is another characteristic. Precious stones are famous for luster, but rock salt is not.

LUSTER
Metallic
Glassy
Resinous
Silky

STREAK
Color of Streak Made by Mineral on Piece of Tile

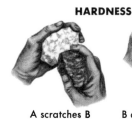

HARDNESS
A scratches B   B does not scratch A

Hardness and heaviness are other traits. Diamonds are the hardest of natural minerals, though relatively light. Bauxite is light but soft. Magnetite, rich in iron, is heavy and magnetic. A few minerals, such as uraninite and carnotite, are radioactive.

Most minerals, when forming from magma or lava, or when left by evaporating water, form crystals. Crystals are exact forms determined by the arrangement of atoms in the molecules that make up the substance. Ice crystals, determined by the physical nature of common water, are among the most beautiful of all.

Crystals of many common substances, such as sugar and salt, can be prepared by dissolving a small quantity in water and then evaporating the water. They are interesting when seen under a microscope.

COLLECTING ROCKS AND MINERALS

Walks, hikes, and vacation trips are the more interesting if one can recognize rocks and minerals. Millions of people make a hobby of identifying, collecting, and cutting and polishing them.

The main kinds of rocks, such as granite, basalt, and shale, are fairly easy to recognize after a little practice. Some minerals can be quickly learned, too, and the forms in which they appear in rocks can be fascinating.

Specimens can be looked for wherever bedrocks are exposed—in road cuts, quarries, mines,

FRACTURE

CONCHOIDAL FRACTURE: OBSIDIAN   UNEVEN FRACTURE: ARSENOPYRITE   EARTHY FRACTURE: CLAY

CLEAVAGE

CUBIC CLEAVAGE: GALENA   RHOMBOHEDRAL CLEAVAGE: CALCITE   BASAL CLEAVAGE: MICA

cliffs, excavations. Streambeds, beaches, glacial moraines, desert areas, and volcanic landscapes also are likely places. In some localities bedrocks may look all the same, but if the strata have been compressed by folding or invaded by magma, interesting specimens may be found. Minerals are likely to occur also where trickles of ground water have deposited them; for instance, quartz crystals in limestone joints.

Certain minerals cannot be identified even by experts without laboratory tests. But, with a guide book to help, anyone can soon learn to identify scores of specimens and thus enjoy them more.

Equipment for a rock collector—*A geologist's hammer, a bag for carrying specimens, and a storage rack or box are indispensable. Other items can be obtained as the collection grows.*

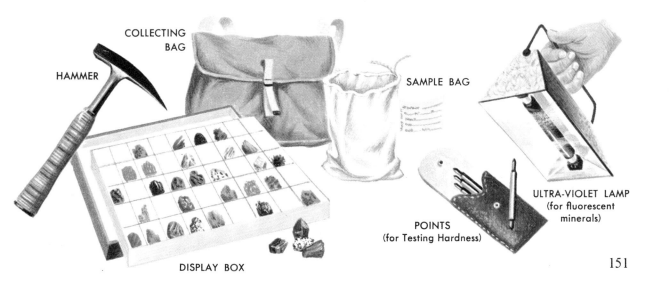

HAMMER   COLLECTING BAG   SAMPLE BAG   ULTRA-VIOLET LAMP (for fluorescent minerals)

POINTS (for Testing Hardness)

DISPLAY BOX

151

Seascapes

THE OCEAN covers two thirds of the globe. Compared to the planet's diameter, the ocean is shallow even where it is deepest. Yet until recently the ocean was a mystery. In 1500, long after mariners had started using the compass, the sea was still considered endless and bottomless. It was the domain of monsters that could swallow ships. It had islands of lodestone that pulled iron nails out of ships and wrecked them. Mariners who sailed too far would drop off the edge of the world.

The first scientific investigation of the ocean came late in the nineteenth century with the voyage of the English ship *Challenger* under Sir C. Wyville Thompson. From 1872 to 1876 the little craft cruised the seven seas, sampling water, tracing currents, dredging up sediments and rocks, finding strange species of plants and animals, and sounding depths to three miles.

Later, scientific ships from other countries made similar voyages. But not until the mid-twentieth century did ocean exploration become a major scientific activity. World War II brought rapid development of highly technical instruments for measuring depths, temperatures, magnetism in the sea floor, and other phenomena. After the war, various universities, with aid from national governments, started systematic investigation of the world ocean.

Deep-sea exploration is directed by scientific agencies such as the Scripps Institution of Oceanography, at La Jolla, California, and the Lamont-Doherty Geological Observatory, at Palisades, New York. Agencies cooperate closely. Small ships are fitted with specialized equipment and, manned by scientists and highly trained crews, go out for months-long exploratory voyages. One of the busiest has been the American ship

The Atlantic's bottom—*A map made from data obtained by soundings shows diverse topography: continental shelves with canyons, ocean floor, deeps, submarine mountains, and the Midatlantic Ridge with its great rift.*

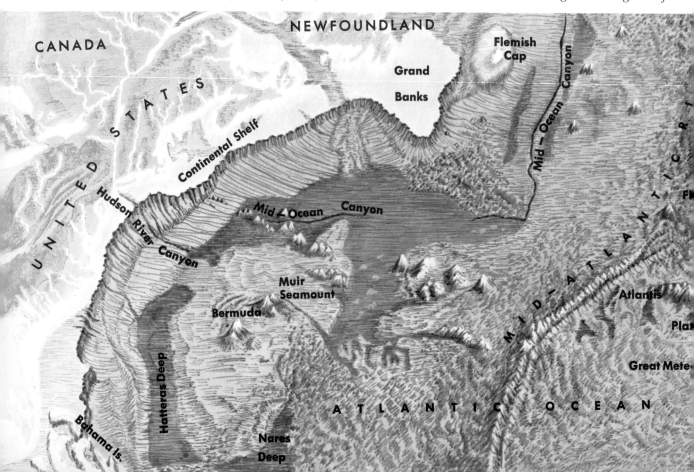

Glomar-Challenger, which in its first five years, ending in 1973, covered 160,000 nautical miles and drilled 450 holes into the sea bottoms at 300 locations.

SOUNDING THE DEPTHS

In the days when depths were measured by means of a rope or wire with a weight on the end, a skipper near land could know whether he had enough water under his keel. But sounding of this sort revealed little about deep ocean bottoms. Today sounding is done with an automatic, continuously working machine which sends shock waves down through the water, records the length of time it takes for the waves to bounce back from the bottom, and—since the speed of sound through salt water is known—translates this information into a depth reading. Given time, a ship can determine bottom contours over a wide area.

Sounding is done also by methods like those used in prospecting for oil and gas. Explosions are set off at the surface. Shock waves rebounding from the sea floor and strata beneath it indicate depth of water, thickness of bottom sediments, kinds and thicknesses of rock strata below sediments, and distance to the mantle.

The unknown sea—*This old print reflects fear of the sea due to ignorance. The true nature of sea bottoms has come to be known only in the 20th century.*

SAMPLING SEA WATER AND SEA BOTTOMS

Besides sounding, scientific ships do much water sampling. A closed cylinder is lowered to a certain depth, opened to allow water to enter, then closed again and raised to the surface. The water is then analyzed for its saltiness, density, and content of living organisms.

Special thermometers for measuring water temperatures are lowered from shipboard to various depths. Temperature changes are clues to sizes and directions of ocean currents, to living conditions for marine life, and to "hot spots" on ocean floors.

An instrument much used for bottom sampling is the "grab." This bucketlike device is dragged over the bottom to pick up samples.

Magnetic sensors are used to test magnetism in the submarine crust. Data obtained indicate types of rock strata and the thickness of the crust. They also show polarization of iron particles in the bedrock. Polarization data indicate movements of ocean-bottom rock that have occurred since the rock formed. Such information is of great value, as our next chapter—on the great crustal plates—will show.

A highly useful exploration tool is the corer, which is essentially a weighted pipe at the end of a long cable. Dropped to the bottom, the corer sinks down into the sediments. Some of these enter the pipe. The unit is then pulled up and the core is removed for analysis. Layers in the core represent the layers of sediment

tialtair

Continental Shelf

FRANCE

PORTUGAL

SPAIN

Madeira

Canary Is.

asin

AFRICA

153

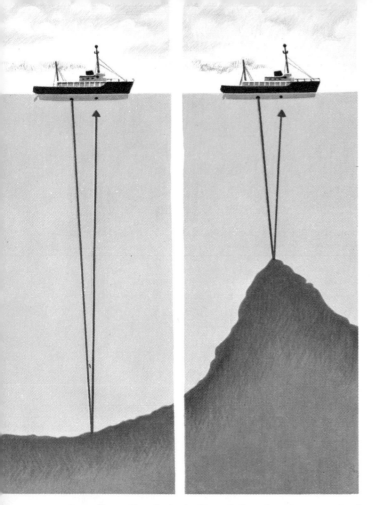

Sounding—*Depth is indicated by the time required for a sound to reach the ocean bottom and return.*

Coring—*Crewmen of a scientific ship lower a small corer. Cores are obtained also by use of drilling rigs.*

on the ocean bottom, from youngest (at the top) to layers that are much older.

Cores of ocean-bottom rock also can be obtained. A drill with a circular bit, shaped like a crown, is operated from the ship by means of a long, rotating cable. As the bit cuts down into the rock, the core moves back into piping behind the bit. Despite the ship's motion on the waves and the enormous twisting strain on so long a cable, operators can direct a drill through more than four miles of water and cut more than 4,000 feet into bedrock.

In relatively shallow water some geologists explore with underwater breathing devices—"scuba." Scuba divers go down to depths of 300 feet.

By means of the bathyscaphe, invented by the French scientist Auguste Piccard, the ocean's darkest deeps can be reached. The bathyscaphe is essentially a sphere of metal and glass built to withstand deep-sea pressures of more than 10 tons per square inch. A powerful light on the bathyscaphe enables the men inside to observe and take pictures through the glass. In 1960 two Americans in a bathyscaphe reached the bottom of the Mariana Trench at 38,400 feet.

ALONG THE CONTINENTAL EDGES

Once the oceans were thought to lie in basins with mostly flat bottoms. Soundings now reveal that the basins are in many ways like landscapes—with mountains and valleys, plains and plateaus, and even volcanoes.

The continental shelves, encountered along edges of most continents, have long been familiar to mariners. These broad, gently sloping platforms run down from the shorelines to depths averaging 500 feet and have an average slope of 10 feet per mile. Beyond the shelf is the continental slope, inclining 150 to 300 feet per mile toward the deep sea floor. The depth of this floor averages about 21,000 feet in the Pacific and 11,000 in the Atlantic, compared to the land's average elevation of about 2,700 feet above sea level.

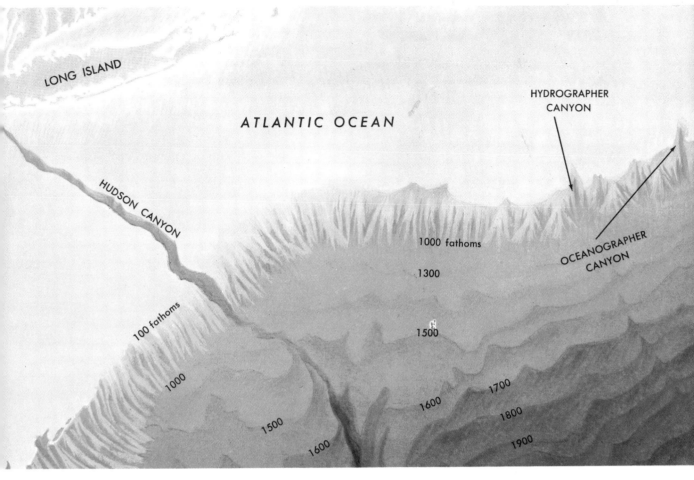

LONG ISLAND

ATLANTIC OCEAN

HYDROGRAPHER CANYON

HUDSON CANYON

1000 fathoms

1300

OCEANOGRAPHER CANYON

100 fathoms

1500

1000

1700

1600

1800

1500

1600

1900

A submerged valley—*The uppermost part of Hudson Canyon was occupied by the Hudson River during the Pleistocene, when sea level was 200 to 300 feet lower. The lower portion probably has been cut by turbidity currents.*

SUBMARINE CANYONS

Continental slopes are laced here and there with gorges called submarine canyons, some of them as deep and nearly as long as Arizona's Grand Canyon. Hudson Gorge, starting in the continental shelf about 10 miles out from the mouth of the Hudson River at New York City, extends 50 miles seaward, reaching 14,000 feet below sea level. A canyon 150 miles long extends from the mouth of Africa's Congo River. La Jolla Canyon, near San Diego, California, about 10 miles long, is one of the best-known submarine canyons because it has been so thoroughly explored and observed by scientists of the Scripps Institution.

Exactly how submarine canyons are cut is not known. Certainly the upper parts, as with Hudson Canyon, were once above sea level and were then being cut by streams or valley glaciers.

During the Pleistocene, so much of Earth's water was locked in glacier ice that ocean levels were 250 to 300 feet below levels of today. But the lower parts of the gorges extend hundreds of feet lower than that. These lower portions were cut probably by turbidity currents—that is, bottom currents loaded with sediments, moving swiftly down the steep continental slopes.

UNDERSEA MOUNTAINS

Much of the ocean floor is fairly level or gently rolling. But here and there, like the land, it has become rumpled into mountain ranges, sunk to great depths, raised into plateaus, cut with valleys, and broken by faults.

Rising from all ocean floors are ranges of volcanic mountains. Some peaks rise above water to form "island arcs," such as the Lesser Antilles in the Atlantic Ocean and the Aleutians

155

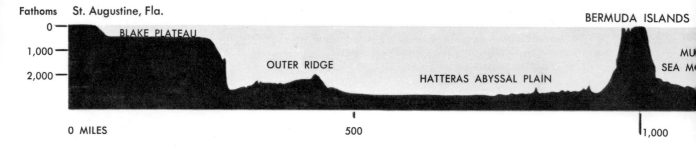

BERMUDA ISLANDS

0

1,000

2,000

BLAKE PLATEAU

OUTER RIDGE

HATTERAS ABYSSAL PLAIN

MU
SEA M

0 MILES

500

1,000

CAPE COD

ATLANTIC

CAPE
HATTERAS

BERMUDA

OCEAN

CUBA

Profile of Atlantic's bottom—*Depth sounding has revealed topography like that of land (considering the vertical exaggeration of 40 to 1). Red line on map (left) shows course of ship that made soundings.*

in the Pacific. Each range is split lengthwise by a long depression, or rift—a zone of earthquakes and volcanic activity. Faults have dislocated segments of the ranges to give them a zigzag aspect. The major ranges link to form a network over the planet (see map, page 158).

The higher ranges are called midocean ridges, because they divide ocean basins approximately down the middle. Lower ranges are known as rises. Lava erupted from fissures and volcanic cones along the ranges spreads out as new ocean floor.

Typical is the Midatlantic Ridge, extending almost from pole to pole. Its loftiest peaks rise above the waves to form Iceland, the Azores, and the Canary Islands. Most other peaks rise about 10,000 feet above the ocean floor and are covered by less than a mile of water.

In the Pacific, a volcanic chain rises six miles to make the Hawaiian Islands. Other ranges form island arcs from the Aleutians to Indonesia.

In these regions earthquakes are frequent and so are volcanic eruptions. The many volcanoes

active in our time include Mauna Loa, Mt. Mayon in the Philippines, Krakatoa in Indonesia, and Katmai in Alaska.

Here and there on the ocean bottoms, especially in the Pacific, are relatively isolated peaks called seamounts. These are all volcanic cones. Some are flat-topped and are called tablemounts, or guyots (GOO-yohz). Probably their tops once rose above sea level and were cut off by wave action. Then, it is thought, the ocean floor beneath the peaks sank because of the removal of supporting lava by eruptions. Thus today some guyot tops are at depths of hundreds of fathoms—far below even the sea levels of Pleistocene times.

CORAL ISLANDS

Many volcanic islands in warm seas are fringed with coral. This consists of masses of hard, sharp-edged limy remains of billions of tiny coral animals and minute organisms called coralline algae.

Where an island has sunk below sea level, or a rise of the sea has covered it, the animals have kept building and thus have created an atoll. This is a ring of coral around a lagoon. Circling some islands are "barrier reefs." Australia's Great Barrier Reef is 1,200 miles long.

Reef-builders are generally active from a little above low-tide level to a depth of about 150 feet. Where sea level has risen since the builders began work, the bottom of the reef may be much deeper—several hundred feet down. Widths of coral reefs range from yards to nearly a mile.

As places of weird rock scenery and the homes of many kinds of ocean life, coral reefs have

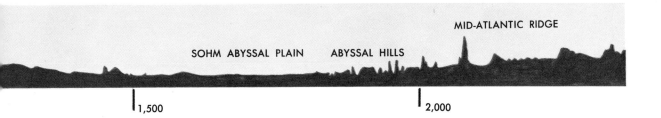

become a paradise for scuba divers. They have also been the graveyards of storm-tossed ships.

DEEPS AND TRENCHES

The ocean floor falls away into low basins, called deeps, 23,000 feet and more beneath the waves. Deeps are wide troughs somewhat like great river valleys. Probably they result from broad crustal movements.

The deepest parts of the ocean bottom are in the trenches, most of which closely parallel island arcs. Trenches are V-shaped in cross section, only about 5 miles wide at the bottom but reaching depths of six or seven miles and extending thousands of miles through the ocean floor. Among the deepest and longest trenches are those near the Mariana Islands, Philippines, Aleutians, and Lesser Antilles. A trench 2,000 miles long runs down the west coast of South America, plunging eight miles below the summits of the Andes.

Near the submarine volcanic chains and trenches the crust is very restless. Beneath the trenches occur the world's deepest, most violent earthquakes, which send out overwhelming tsunamis. It is near the midocean ridges and trenches that most of the active volcanoes of our time are performing.

THE UNDERWATER TREASURY

Within a few decades the sea bottoms have yielded knowledge far beyond expectations.

Ocean depths and bottom contours, directions of ocean currents, and varying temperature conditions are important to shipping and fisheries, and to studies of world weather and climates. Data on ocean depths, currents, and tempera-

tures are vital for naval operations. Oil has been discovered beneath the continental shelves, and there are the rich mineral deposits on sea bottoms near the ridges.

Most important for scientists is what sea bottoms tell about Earth's past and present evolution. Cores supply missing pieces for the jigsaw puzzle of Earth history. Remains of plants and animals help paleontologists to trace the travels of species over land and sea long ago. Fossils in sediments and solid rock are clues to ancient climates—to past glacial ages and periods of high humidity or aridity. Fossils, magnetic data, and radioactive ages of ocean-bottom rocks help scientists to map past movements of continents, as the next chapter explains.

Drilling equipment and engineering skills continue to improve. Some day scientists may drill all the way through the crust, through the Mohorovičić Discontinuity (the thin layer beneath the crust), and into the mantle. The cores will tell what the mantle is made of and indicate how and when the crust formed and how it has moved over the mantle through the ages.

An island of coral—*Swain's Island, in the southwest Pacific, is an atoll. Around the center is the lagoon, and around this the reef, on which waves are breaking.*

157

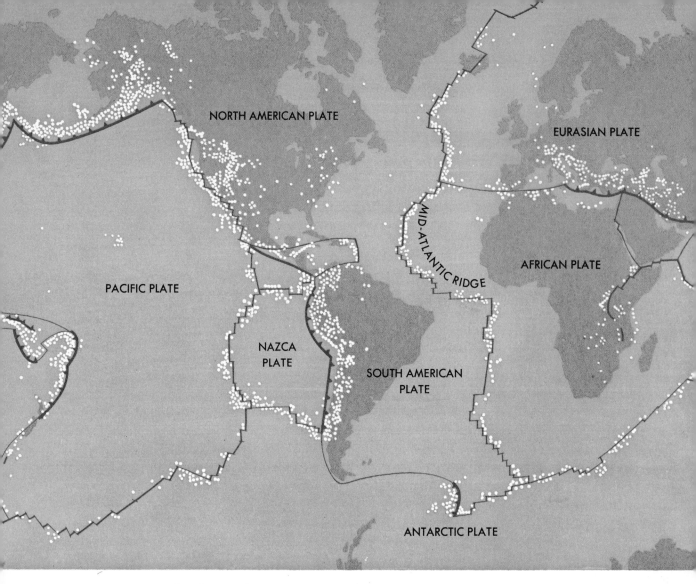

Earth's plates and their boundaries—*Plate boundaries are zones of seismic activity. The white dots indicate epicenters of major earthquakes.*

Wandering Plates

IF any parts of Earth were immovable, surely they would be the continents. These huge, rough blocks include nearly all lands of the planet. Continent "roots" go 30 to 35 miles down into the crust. It is hard to imagine continents moving like great barges through the solid crust.

Fanciful tales of the past tell of moving islands, mountains, and seas. But perhaps the first man of science to suspect that large land masses do move was the English philosopher Sir Francis Bacon. About 1620 he commented that Africa's west coast and South America's east coast would make a good fit. Had the two continents once been a single land mass? Bacon wondered. But science in those days lacked the

information to deal with such questions. Typical was the explanation offered in 1658 by a French writer, R. F. François Plaut. He said the two continents were lands split apart by Noah's Flood.

In 1858 important news came from the French scientist Antonio Snider. Fossils and plants in European coal deposits, he reported, are like those in North America's Appalachian region. Perhaps Europe and North America were once joined!

In 1915 a German geophysicist, Alfred Wegener, came up with a well-argued theory. He said most of the continents, if brought together into a single land mass, would fit better

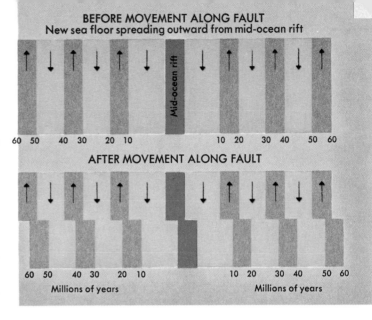

BEFORE MOVEMENT ALONG FAULT
New sea floor spreading outward from mid-ocean rift

AFTER MOVEMENT ALONG FAULT

Millions of years

An area of sea floor before and after movement along a cross fault—*Arrow in each band shows polarity. Each band is dated by radioactivity and fossils.*

than they could if formed independently. He pointed to the similarity of Paleozoic New World fossils (those over 200 million years old) to those of the Old World. He observed that some lands which are now warm, such as Brazil and the Congo, show evidence of ancient glaciers. Therefore, Wegener argued, if the north and south poles have not moved, South America and Africa *have* moved. But Wegener could not explain how "continental drift" could occur.

TELLTALE SEA BOTTOMS

After World War II came the era of ocean-bottom exploration.

One significant finding was that the age of the oldest sea bottoms, as indicated by radioactive dating and fossil ages, is about 180 million years. The continents had yielded samples with ages of over three billion years. Why should sea bottoms be so young?

The youngest bottom rock was found along the midocean ridges. As samples were taken farther and farther from the ridges, the older they became, with few exceptions. Scientists decided new ocean floor is being made continually along the ridges as lava is erupted and spreads outward somewhat like a conveyor belt.

"Sea-floor spreading" was indicated by magnetic data also. When lava flows from a rift, iron particles in it become magnetized with reference to Earth's magnetic poles and "freeze" in the north-south position as the lava solidifies. As the lava rock moves away from the rift in both directions over millions of years, the polarity of Earth reverses (the north and south poles interchange) many times. Therefore, going away from a rift, scientists would find a band or strip of sea bottom with one polarity, then one with the other polarity, next a band with the opposite polarity, and so on. These

bands when marked on a map suggested zebra stripes. However, many were broken and offset by faults. A band would go so far, then be interrupted at a fault line. On the other side of the line the band would be shifted to one side or the other. By analyzing these shifts, scientists could determine how far and in what directions parts of the sea floor had moved. Further, because sea-floor rock could be dated by means of radioactivity tests, the movements themselves could be dated.

Even fossils testified to sea-floor movements. In the north Pacific, sediments were found to contain fossils of types native only to the equatorial regions. The fossils were about 65 million years old. In that time the floor of the Pacific had moved north more than 1,800 miles. Nor was this movement of the Pacific floor an exception: fossils elsewhere indicated past movements in all ocean bottoms.

A **wandering pole**—*Yellow area shows limits within which the north pole apparently wandered 270 to 230 million years ago.*

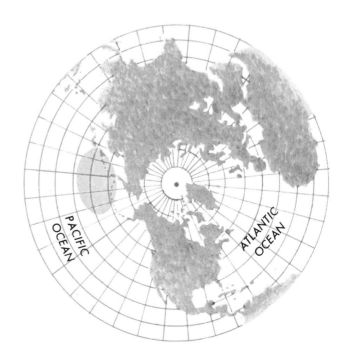

PACIFIC OCEAN

ATLANTIC OCEAN

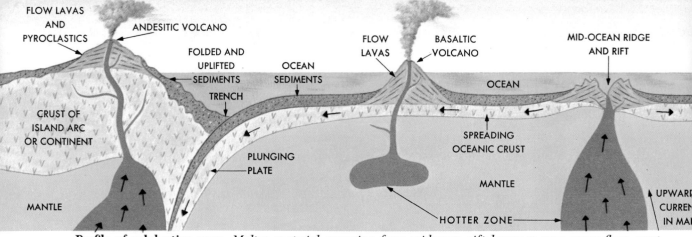

Profile of subduction zone—*Molten material emerging from midocean rift becomes new ocean-floor crust, which moves away from rift. At or near edge of continent, this crust plunges down into mantle. A trench develops where it goes down. Beyond the trench, mountains are produced by thrusting forces.*

Investigators now faced a question. If new sea floor keeps spreading, where does it go?

The answer, or part of it, was found in the ocean trenches. Magnetic, age, and fossil data showed that sea floor moves toward a trench, descends as one side of it, and disappears under the other side. The opposite side is rock of a different type and a different age. Evidently sea floor plunges down into the mantle.

Scientists now realized why the oldest sea-bottom rock is relatively young. Older sea floor has been swallowed up in the mantle. The trenches are "subduction zones"—that is, crustal breaks where ocean floor is pushing down. No wonder trenches are hot, shaken by earthquakes, and bordered by volcanoes.

TELLTALE CONTINENTAL ROCKS

Now another question was asked: If sea floors can move, why not continents?

Bedrocks of all continents were tested for polarity. A world map was marked with arrows to show polarities of rocks of the Permian Period, ending some 230 million years ago. Arrows on different continents mostly disagreed as to the locations of Earth's magnetic poles. Arrows within any one continent agreed roughly, but indicated pole locations different from today's.

Next, the continents were cut out of the map and fitted together as closely as possible. Now nearly all arrows—including all the continents—pointed to approximately the same pole locations. Here was a strong suggestion that during the Permian Period continents were united.

Meanwhile rock structures of the New and Old Worlds were compared. Remarkable similarities were found between the Appalachians of North America and the mountains of Great Britain and Scandinavia in regard to folds and the order of rock layers of different types. Strong likenesses were seen also between the Appalachians and Africa's Atlas Mountains. Significantly, these similarities were in rocks of the Paleozoic Era (which ended with the Permian Period) and early Mesozoic Era up to about 180 million years ago. Here was evidence of a world continent existing until the early Mesozoic!

Close similarities were found in Paleozoic fossils, also. Paleontologists agree that animals and plants on an isolated land mass evolve by a succession of generations into unique forms. If the continents had always been separate, close similarities between fossils would have been virtually impossible. But the similarities in Paleozoic fossils were clear. They were the more significant because in fossils younger than around 200 million years similarities were less common. According to fossils, the Old and New Worlds split some 200 million years ago.

At this point the age of the oldest rock samples from the ocean bottom—180 million years—became dramatically important. It strongly suggested that present ocean bottoms started forming 180 million years ago when a world continent was breaking up. "Continental drift" had occurred while ocean floor was being made.

A GRAND PATTERN APPEARS

Scientists now began to piece together a grand pattern of Earth changes. The crust, they saw, is divided into broad plates. Some plates consist entirely of sea-bottom crust; others combine sea-bottom and continental crust. All plates are slowly moving. Some are "rafting" the continents.

Where plates are colliding beneath the ocean, one turns down beneath the other and is consumed in the mantle. Where plates collide along a land-sea boundary, the sea-bottom edge turns down because sea-bottom crust, being basaltic, is slightly heavier than continental crust, which is more granitic and sedimentary. Again a trench and mountains are created.

Where colliding plate edges are both continental, neither turns down, and the result is extreme folding and uplift—an "accordioning" of crust. Where one plate simply glances off another, there is earthquake activity and perhaps some mountain building, but less disturbance than is likely to result from head-on collisions.

In this pattern geologists saw not only the nature of continental drift—or, more precisely, plate drift—but also the origin of mountains. Deep fractures along which volcanic mountains develop are in most instances boundaries between plates. Geosynclines, the "cradles" of fold mountains, start as trenches, in which sediments rise because of their relative lightness compared to the basalt of the deep crust or because of collision pressure—or both. Block mountains could be expected to develop where continents are moving apart or are in a tangential, or glancing, collision.

The pattern did present problems. One was the existence of mountain ranges such as the American Rockies and the Russian Urals far from the borders of plates as these were mapped. Perhaps such ranges were created as plates collided; then plate motion stopped and the breaks were "healed," forming "sutures." Another problem was the existence of the Hawaiian Islands in the middle of the Pacific Plate—not near a border. Here a possible explanation was that a hot current of mantle material, rising like a plume beneath the plate, had broken through. Plumes seemed to be an explanation also for broad uplifts within plates, such as the Colorado Plateau.

PANGEA: WORLD CONTINENT
Clear evidence of plate drift went back 200 million years at most. Between that date and the date of the oldest known rocks (3.76 billion years) there had been plenty of time for crust to form, break up, and re-form—again and again. Scientists realized that the early history of the crust would never be known, but they could agree on events of the more recent past.

Some 200 million years ago a world continent, Pangea (pan-JEE-uh) (Greek: "all earth"), began breaking up into two masses, Laurasia in the north and Gondwanaland in the south. As tens of millions of years passed, Laurasia

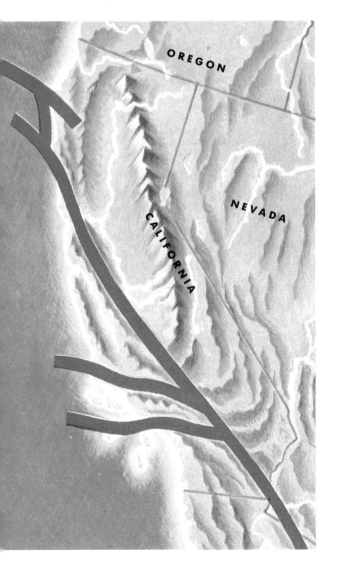

Where two plates meet: *California's San Andreas fault (longest red band) and associated faults mark the zone along which the northwest-moving Pacific Plate is glancing off the North American Plate.*

161

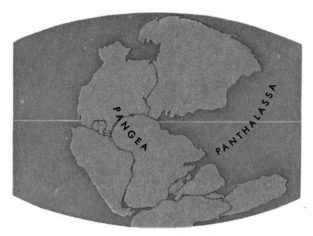

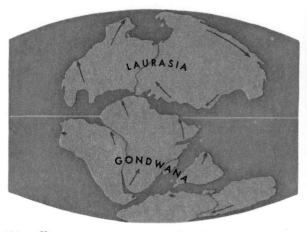

PROBABLE HISTORY OF CONTINENTAL DRIFT—200 million years ago: *The universal continent Pangea, in the universal ocean Panthalassa, is divided by great rifts into seven major parts.*

180 million years ago: *Pangea has been breaking up to form Laurasia and Gondwana. The lands are drifting westward. The Atlantic Ocean is beginning to form, and the Tethys Sea is closing up.*

broke up to make Europe and Asia in the east, North America in the west. Gondwanaland came apart to make Africa, India, Australia, Antarctica, and South America. Today the plates that carry these land masses are still drifting, and there is every reason to suppose that they will drift for millions of years to come.

THE PLATES TODAY

In our time the Pacific Plate, the largest, is growing mainly by volcanic eruptions along the Pacific-Antarctic Ridge and the East Pacific Rise. Pacific sea bottom is plunging into the mantle mostly on the north and west sides of the plate. Trenches and volcanic mountains border the Pacific Plate from the Aleutians down through the Japanese and Philippine Islands to Indonesia and New Zealand.

In the northeast the Pacific Plate is glancing off the North American Plate. The boundary between them splits California from a point north of San Francisco down into the Gulf of California. Part of this boundary is the notorious San Andreas Fault, along which the land on the west (Pacific Plate) side has moved northwest several hundred miles during the past 10 million years. The Gulf of California and the Salton Trough are parts of an opening rift valley between the plates.

Farther south, the Pacific Plate is bordered by the Cocos and Nazca Plates. These are

growing by volcanic activity along the East Pacific and Chile Rises. On the eastern sides of these plates the sea floor is going down under Central America and South America, rumpling the crust to form Central America's volcanic highlands and South America's Andes. These volcanoes along the eastern side of the Pacific Ocean complete the "ring of fire."

The North and South American plates are growing along their eastern edges by eruptions from the Midatlantic Ridge. The lavas form Iceland (which is split neatly by the ridge) and scattered islands to the south, including the Canaries and Azores. Atlantic Ocean floor is plunging in the Puerto Rico Trench, accounting for the build-up of volcanic islands in the Caribbean area. The sea floor is going down also in the Antarctic.

The African and Eurasian Plates are colliding between Gibraltar and the Himalayas, pushing up the Alpine-Himalayan mountain system and causing earthquakes and volcanic activity in the vicinity. The Mediterranean Sea is a remnant of the Tethys Sea, which once divided Europe and Asia from Africa. At the northeastern side of the African Plate, east of the Mediterranean, sea floor is plunging. Also in the northeast a part of the African Plate is breaking away, leaving widening gaps. One of these gaps is partly filled by the Red Sea. Another forms the African Rift Valley—

135 million years ago: *The Atlantic and Indian oceans are widening, South America is breaking away from Africa, and India is moving relatively rapidly toward Asia.*

65 million years ago: *The Atlantic has opened wide. South America is free from Africa. North and South America are still separate. The Tethys Sea has become almost closed to become the Mediterranean.*

the chain of depressions, partly filled with lakes and also a zone of volcanic activity, extending from Palestine to Rhodesia.

WHY DO THEY MOVE?

Most scientists agree that the plates "float" on the mantle and that Earth's heat helps to keep them moving. Perhaps warm convection currents in the mantle push the crust up here and there, and cold currents drag it down. A plate may rise on a plume of mantle material, then slide off.

The mantle is nearly plastic, the crust relatively rigid. Therefore the crust may lag behind the mantle—slipping on it a little—as Earth rotates. That could account for the tendency of plates to drift more westward than otherwise.

Another possible cause of drift is the gravitational pulls of Moon and Sun. Still another is the re-balancing of crust as rising magma adds to its bulk, and as erosion wastes are transported from highlands toward the sea.

A few have argued that the crust was broken up when a large celestial body—the planet Venus, or perhaps a comet—passed near Earth and disrupted it by gravitational attraction. Most scientists, however, say this could not have occurred according to physical laws as now known. They prefer to look for causes in everyday events that can be observed rather than in unlikely catastrophes of the past.

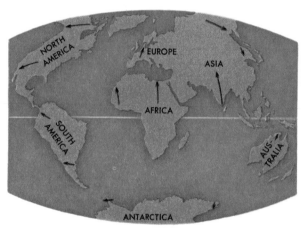

Today: *North and South America are joined and split off completely from the other continents. India has collided with southern Asia. Australia has moved rapidly away from Antarctica. Westward drift has continued.*

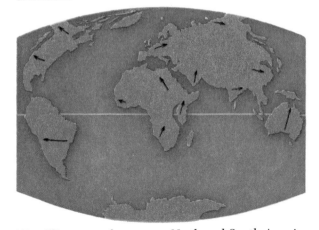

50 million years from now: *North and South America will probably have moved farther west. Part of East Africa will have broken off and moved northeast. Australia also will have moved northeast.*

On the Moon: *The astronauts explored a world that was fascinating, yet showed much less geologic diversity than Earth does.*

Beyond Earth

PROBABLY no one ever really believed the Moon to be made of green cheese, but the human imagination has produced remarkable ideas about it. In mythology the Moon was a god or goddess, or a chariot, or the home of a godly being. As recently as a century ago, most people were sure the Moon must be a place of weird landscapes with even weirder inhabitants.

The first scientific lunar observer was the Italian genius Galileo, who in 1610 trained his homemade 30-power telescope on the Moon and viewed "another world." After Galileo, astronomers built up much physical information about the Moon—its movement around Earth (27 days 7 hours 43 minutes), its varying distance from Earth (221,460 to 252,710 miles), its diameter (2,160 miles), its gravity (one sixth of Earth's). Our satellite was recognized as airless and waterless, with a surface shaped by volcanic eruptions and meteorite impacts.

After direct lunar exploration started in the 1960s, previous scientific ideas were found to be mostly correct, but much new information was obtained. Contrary to fears that landing craft would sink out of sight in Moondust, all landings were safe. Space-suited explorers ranged over the lunar landscape afoot and in small electric automobiles. They saw and photographed Galileo's "other world"—a barren and dry land strewn with broken rock. No streams were seen—no evidence of any water, past or present. The astronauts collected bagfuls of rocks, gathered data on temperatures, moonquakes, gravity, elevations, and other matters, and returned to the friendly green Earth.

Scientists in laboratories studied reports and photographs, and analyzed rock samples and instrumental data. Rocks were mostly varieties of basalt along with a feldspar-rich gabbro called anorthosite—more common on the Moon than on Earth. Lunar craters were confirmed as made by volcanic activity and impacts. The maria ("seas") were recognized as widespreading flows of lava erupted from the lunar interior after collisions with large meteorites or asteroids. The winding trenches called rilles, long a puzzle to lunar observers at telescopes, were seen to be flow lines on lava. Mountains, grabens, and numerous fault scarps were results of volcanism and crustal movements, especially movements due to impacts.

Naturally occurring lunar quakes, produced by changes in Earth's gravity pull, were weak. Their depths—up to about 700 miles—indicated a rigid mantle beneath the crust, and a partly melted core about 900 miles in diameter.

Gravity data suggested a crust thinner on the side of the Moon that faces Earth, perhaps explaining why this side shows more maria—the huge lava flows produced by impacts.

No lunar rock sample had any trace of organic compounds essential to life.

The radioactive age of the oldest lunar rock brought back was 3.9 billion years. Some rocks tested older but falsely so—their radioactive "clocks" had been upset by disturbances.

Scientists decided the Moon must have formed, like Earth and other planets, about 4.6 billion years ago by clustering of material in a cloud swirling around the young Sun. For 600 million years heat from radioactivity and impacts melted the lunar interior, allowing iron-rich minerals to sink and form a core while silicates, being lighter, formed a crust. Then came some 800 million years of cataclysmic events due perhaps to a climax in radioactive heating and a prolonged shower of big meteorites or asteroids. Thus was produced most of the landscape we see today.

The age of the youngest rock sample, 3.0 billion years, indicated that since the cataclysmic period little has happened on the Moon except slow weathering by temperature changes and bombardment by small meteorites.

While astronauts tramped the Moon, space ships raced toward Venus, Mars, Mercury, and Jupiter. In these unmanned voyages, cameras took thousands of photographs. Other instruments recorded temperatures, radiation, magnetism, light reflection, and other phenomena.

Mars was revealed as a planet with mountains, large grabens, plains with vast dust storms, and thin sheets of ice near the poles. Valleys with tributaries indicated stream erosion, but no water was visible—nor any sign of the legendary Martian "canals." One side of Mars was seen to be much cratered, like the Moon; the other suggested Earth's ocean bottoms, with their plains, rises, and ridges. Olympus Mons, over 100 miles wide, was rated the largest shield volcano in the solar system.

Spacecraft have added little to existing geologic information about Venus. Radar sounding has indicated a mountainous, cratered landscape, blistering hot under the heat-trapping cloud cover. Spacecraft photographs of Mercury revealed a Moon-like landscape, probably hot enough to melt lead. Data from a "fly-by" of Jupiter confirmed existing ideas of ice clouds thousands of miles thick, covering a solid ice ball with a rocky or iron core.

These first ventures of astrogeology, the geology of celestial bodies, seem to prove that the nature of the celestial bodies is consistent with the nature of Earth. Although the forms produced by nature are infinite in variety, and often strange to us, the processes of nature everywhere are basically the same.

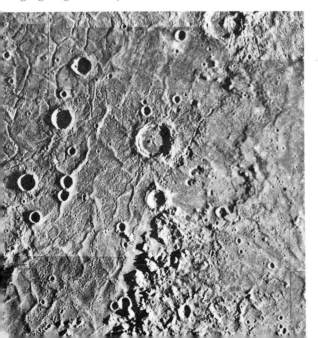

Mercurian landscape—*Mariner 10 photo shows Moon-like terrain: mile-high mountains, impact craters, zigzag ridges and rifts. Area is 260 miles wide.*

Martian landscape: *Mariner 9 photo, made 1,051 miles from Mars, shows impact craters and part of valley made by a stream or possibly a lava flow.*

Almost too strange to believe: *Children in a museum, although accustomed to seeing dinosaur skeletons, still gaze in wonderment. Even paleontologists find it hard to grasp the enormous span of geologic time, and they too marvel at the strangeness of the plants and animals that have inhabited our Earth.*

Graveyards

EARTH'S crust is a vast graveyard. Here lie scattered the remains of living things that have roamed our planet or grown in its soils for three thousand million years. These relics are entombed in sedimentary rocks of mountains and sea bottoms, in the sands of deserts, beneath the grass of meadows. They are washed by the rains, frozen in ice, baked by the Sun, and blown by wind. We cannot pick up a handful of soil anywhere in the world without lifting with it some atoms of a being that once knew the Sun and the rain.

TRACES OF VANISHED LIFE

Traces of ancient living things found in rock are known as fossils. Most have lain in rock for millions of years; erosion has gradually uncovered them. They appear in walls of canyons, in bedrock on mountain slopes, in roadcuts, on rock floors of streams, in coal beds and in quarries. There is a good chance of seeing fossils in most places where there are sedimentary rocks.

Some ancient Greek philosophers suspected the true nature of fossils, but they were not

Spirit writings?—*Fossils and odd mineral specimens were once believed to be the work of underground spirits. These drawings from Kircher's* Mundus Subterraneus *were said to be from specimens actually found.*

sure. For centuries afterward, through the Middle Ages, odd ideas about fossils prevailed. Typical was the notion that they are writings or charms of underground spirits.

In the fifteenth century Leonardo da Vinci noted correctly the origin of sedimentary rocks. He was aware that fossils are traces of ancient life. Yet even by the mid-1700s educated people believed fossils to be remains of plants and animals buried in the mud of Noah's Flood, just a few thousand years earlier.

By 1750 a few naturalists such as Jean Guettard (who called attention to the extinct volcanoes in southern France) had noticed that fossils are mostly different in structure from today's life forms. Personal observation was beginning to convince them that most fossils are much older than a few thousand years. Perhaps fossils dated from long ages before Noah's Flood!

Soon after 1800 this line of thought was developed by the French naturalist Georges Cuvier. He noticed that fossils of a certain group —shellfish, for example—in any one rock stratum often differ markedly from corresponding fossils in strata above and below. Earth history, he suspected, is divided into stages in which different sets of animals and plants gradually developed.

In England about the same time a surveyor named William Smith was studying sedimentary rocks. Where strata are "stacked up," he reasoned, the layer at the top must be the one that formed most recently. Going down, the strata must become older. This principle of Smith's became known as the law of super-

position. It applies where the rock strata have not been overturned.

Smith saw that fossils can be clues to relative ages of rocks. For example, if a certain kind of shellfish fossil is found in a stratum near London, and a fossil exactly like it is found in a stratum 100 miles away, these strata must be of about the same age—even if the stratum at one place is near the top of the "stack" and the stratum at the other place is near the bottom.

Tramping over England, mapping rock formations and checking fossils, Smith prepared the way for Sir Charles Lyell. Lyell, a very good writer, spread the growing knowledge of geology widely among scientists and other educated people. Traveling all over Europe, he studied the folded and faulted Alps, volcanoes old and new, changing sea levels, evidences of weathering and erosion, patterns of rock stratification, and fossils. In all these things he saw a connected story of the past.

20 million years old—*This fossil leaf of a gingko plant was found in shale near Grand Coulee Dam in Washington. The original leaf was green.*

167

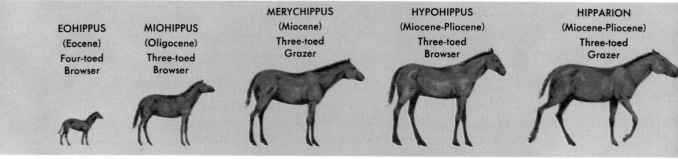

Horses then and now—*The forms and relative sizes of these horses, beginning with primitive Eohippus at left, span 50 million years.*

THE PARADE OF LIFE

By the mid-1800s most geologists realized that prehistoric life forms had changed gradually from generation to generation, over long ages. But how had changes occurred?

An answer was given in the historic book *The Origin of Species,* published in 1858 by the English naturalist Charles Darwin. New physical traits, said Darwin, appear in living things from generation to generation. Traits that help in the battle for existence continue in a species because the individuals have a better chance to survive and to have offspring. Traits that are not useful tend to disappear. Thus the procession of life keeps changing. Over millions of years, for example, the fish form leads to the amphibian form, the amphibian to the reptile, the reptile to the mammal. Some changes are "improvements"; most are not.

Like other naturalists of his time, Darwin half-believed that traits are developed by individuals according to need, then passed along to offspring. Biologists have since learned that new traits are due to changes in genes—units of heredity passed along from generation to generation. Changes in genes are apparently random and do not result from an individual's behavior or experience.

Darwin's theory of "natural selection" started science on its way to an understanding of processes that changed life through the ages. Today, when we look at a fossil, we know it is not just a meaningless relic but rather a link in one of the long chains of life.

THE MAKING OF FOSSILS

In our imagination let us travel 400 million years back into the past.

On a sea bottom a little animal called a trilobite—somewhat like our horseshoe crab—dies. Before it can be eaten by another animal an ocean current covers it with sand.

Hundreds of years pass. The slow trickling of water through the trilobite's remains carries these away, bit by bit. The weight of sand above gradually closes the space. At last nothing is left of the trilobite but an imprint, buried deep in sand that is gradually turning to sandstone.

Millions of years go by. The sea bottom rises, higher and higher, until it is a mountain

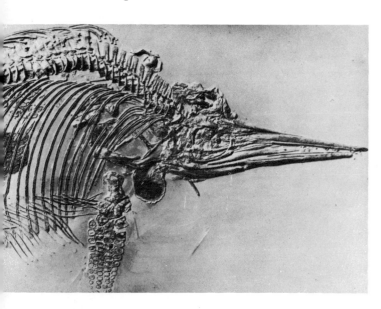

The head of a "fish-lizard"—*In this 160-million-year-old fossil ichthyosaur are preserved not only imprints of body parts but also actual bones.*

EQUUS
(Modern)
Single-toed Grazer

range. Today, 400 million years after the trilobite died, a stone image of it lies in the bedrock of the Canadian Rockies, 14,000 feet above the sea.

Now go back 180 million years to the region that is now Connecticut. Swift streams are eroding mountains nearby, carrying red earth down to the lowlands. Walking on its hind legs along a muddy bank is an early dinosaur, *Anchisaurus*. This slender, speedy reptile, seven or eight feet long, is leaving birdlike tracks.

The next day, a rain in the mountains causes the stream to flood over its banks a little—enough to fill some of the tracks with new sand. Millions of years pass and the tracks are buried under red sandstone and shale many hundreds of feet deep.

At last it is the twentieth century. Erosion in the Connecticut Valley has uncovered the ancient tracks. And—who knows?—these exposed tracks may be noticed by a geologist on a fossil hunt, or a family on a picnic.

Now look back 250 million years. The sea, creeping up from the Gulf of Mexico, has covered part of the Mississippi Valley. Along its eastern shores are swamps where coal for the future is being made. On its bottoms limestones are forming.

Ages pass—a span 120,000 times as long as the Christian era. The sea bottom is now dry land. Man, a newcomer on the planet, has opened quarries in the limestones and is cutting out thousands of blocks for building stone. This is shipped all over the country for use in churches and other fine buildings. Some of it, if you look closely, is seen to be packed with shells—a curious end for creatures that lived on sea bottoms 250 million years ago!

The bodies of most living things are destroyed and the remains scattered soon after death. The chance that any one animal or plant will be preserved as a fossil may be one in a million.

Even so, fossils are vast in number and variety. Sea bottoms entombed not only trilobites and shellfish but seaweeds, fishes, scorpions, worms and their burrows, sea reptiles, corals, and other forms by the billion, including types existing today and types long since vanished. Strata formed beneath lakes and streams, and by wind-blown desert sands, yield the earliest land plants, the first amphibians and birds, tree ferns and dinosaurs, insects and mammals and all the rest. Many fossils are simply imprints of bodies, skin, bones, or shells, and some are hard parts of the original animals—actual bones and shells.

Some fossils, such as the fallen trees in the Petrified Forest of Arizona, still show original body structures. Water has filtered through the remains and replaced them with minerals which preserve very fine structural details.

Many fossils are casts. Rock waste has filled the hollow left by decay of the plant or animal. Still other fossils are seen only as a faint color pattern on a rock surface.

Some pieces of shale split so as to reveal thin layers of a black material inside. This is carbon left from decay of organic tissues.

Some sedimentary rocks yield few fossils or none. Shale formed from mud of a fresh-water lake bottom before life existed outside the ocean would have no plant or animal fossils, though it might have ripple marks made by waves. A limestone formed mainly by minerals precipitated from sea water may offer few fossils. Fossils can be destroyed by water trickling between rock grains, or by heat and pressure.

DETECTIVE WORK WITH FOSSILS

Most fossils are just bits and pieces. The few whole ones are often twisted, crumpled, and flattened. Making sense out of such remains is a job for the experts known as paleontologists. (The name comes from the Greek words meaning "ancient," "things," and "study.") Paleon-

tologists explore for fossils, dig them out, treat them with preservatives if necessary, and ship them back to laboratories. There experts examine them with microscopes, test them chemically, slice them into thin sheets to reveal their inner structures, put the various pieces together, compare them with other fossils and modern life forms, and discuss them with other experts.

Removal of fossils from rock slabs must be done with great care. Some fossils, such as bone, may fall to pieces when exposed to air.

Even a tiny piece of fossil—a bit of bone, part of a leaf imprint—may be an important clue to the nature of an ancient plant or animal. From bits of fossils paleontologists can sometimes tell what the original living thing was. But it is not true that an expert can take a single bone of an unknown animal and, with this alone to guide him, construct a skeleton like that of the original animal. That has been tried a few times—with fantastic results!

Ticklish work—*Freeing perishable remains such as bone or skin from rock demands great skill and care.*

UNVEILING FORMER WORLDS

The fossils in a sedimentary stratum represent, more or less, the community of animals and plants that were living in the region when the sediments were laid down. The characteristics of the rock itself—whether limestone, shale, or sandstone—indicate whether the sediments were laid down on a sea floor, in a swamp, in a desert, or on a riverbed. By putting together all the clues, the scientist puts together pictures of ancient environments.

In certain shale formations in Wyoming, for example, the paleontologist finds bones of the clumsy, 65-foot dinosaur *Brontosaurus.* In strata of about the same age are remains of dragonflies, cockroaches, fishes, and winged reptiles known as pterosaurs. The abundant plant remains include rushes and tree ferns—types that flourish in swamps. Thus the paleontologist, detail by detail, reads the story of *Brontosaurus,* his animal and plant neighbors, and the swamps where they lived long ago.

The geologist usually can assume, as William Smith did, that the stratum he is studying is younger than any one below it and older than any above it, unless there are signs of overturning. The order of strata thus indicates the chronological order in which ancient life forms

appeared. In a single cliff there may be the record of several million years. Following the strata from bottom to top, the geologist might find evidence of how the animals, plants, and their environments in this region evolved during the ages of history represented by the strata. Thus the Wyoming shale layers, from bottom to top, could show how the swamp where *Brontosaurus* lived dried up, the climate became cooler, and new types of plants and animals replaced the old ones.

FOSSILS: KEYS TO AGE

Reconstructing the past by studying rock strata is difficult. No region contains a complete history in the rocks. From most areas some or all sedimentary strata—if any—that existed in the past have been eroded away. In mountains, strata have often been cracked, tilted, folded, sunk, raised, pushed out of line, inverted, and jumbled. Some rock masses lie too deep to be observed. Every region with sedimentary rocks has them in different amounts and different combinations. Wherever the geologist starts "reading" a formation, he faces a new problem.

One key to that problem, as William Smith showed, is the geologist's knowledge of fossils. In any stratum containing fossils, the fossil types indicate which period of Earth history the stratum represents.

Suppose a sandstone stratum in a Wisconsin hill is found to contain the same kinds of trilobites that are found in a certain sandstone stratum in the Canadian Rockies. The two sandstones, it can be assumed, were laid down during about the same period. This is so even if the strata just above and just below the Wisconsin stratum yield fossils different from the strata just above and below the Canadian stratum. In this way, fossils serve as keys to the relative ages of sedimentary strata all over the world.

Further, the ages of sedimentary strata may indicate ages of strata next to them. Suppose a paleontologist finds a lava flow between two sandstone strata. The fossils in these strata are of the same types. The paleontologist concludes

Putting Tyrannosaurus rex together—*Fossil skeletons may be jumbled when discovered, with bones of different animals mixed in. Sorting and reconstruction may be a task requiring many months.*

that the lava is approximately of the same age as the sandstone, even though the lava contains no fossils.

EXACTLY HOW LONG AGO?

Ordinarily the geologist is concerned about relative ages of strata, not absolute ages. He needs to know not whether a certain stratum is exactly 56 million years old, for example, but what geologic period it belongs to—that is, where it fits into Earth history. Naturally he would like to know how long the stratum took to form and when this happened. But in most cases this is hard to determine. Sediments pile up at different rates, even in the same place. Erosion rates, changes in animal and plant forms, episodes of volcanic activity—these offer few clues to calendar dates.

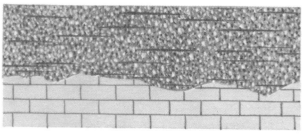

FORMATION 1

FORMATION 2

Where absolute dates—dates in years—are needed, the geologist can now turn to radiometric dating.

Radioactivity is, as we know, the process by which certain chemical elements spontaneously emit energy and thus break down to become more stable elements. Each radioactive element has its own rate of breakdown, which is designated as its "half-life"—the time required for half of any quantity of the element to change into the stable element. Thus uranium-238, breaking down to lead-206, has a half-life of 4.5 billion years. Potassium-40, breaking down to argon-40, has a half-life of 1.8 billion years. Stages of breakdown can be used as yardsticks to measure ages of rocks and sediments.

Consider, for example, a lava flow. As the flow cools, the mineral uraninite, containing uranium-238, forms in it. At the moment of formation uranium starts breaking down thus:

Years Elapsed (billions)	Uranium-238 Changed to Lead
0	0
1.125	22.22%
2.250	33.33
4.5	50.00

Therefore, if a sample from the lava flow indicates that about 22 per cent of the uranium-238 in it has turned to lead, the lava's age must be about 1.125 billion (1,125,000,000) years.

Gaps in the geologic story—*Sedimentary strata in succession usually are parallel, showing continuous deposition. But on occasion the geologist notices a break in continuity between an older and a younger layer. This may indicate a period of erosion, or perhaps earth movements, after the older layer was deposited. If the layers are parallel, the break is called a disconformity; if not parallel, an angular unconformity.*

A few paragraphs ago we saw how a geologist found the relative age of a lava flow by discovering nearly identical fossils in sandstone strata just above and below it. The fossils did not give the date of the lava in years, but radioactive dating could.

The radiometric date would not necessarily be very accurate for the sandstone. The geologist would not know how much time passed between

A rock puzzle—*These opposite outcrops, 100 miles apart, present a typical problem in stratigraphy—the study of rock strata relative to one another. The strata appear to match, except that 1a and 4 are missing. Were 1a and 4 eroded away? Or were they never deposited at all? Radioactive dating and index fossils (if any are present in the strata) could give the answers.*

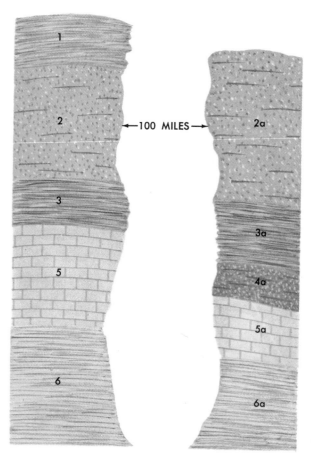

the formation of the lower sandstone stratum and the occurrence of the lava flow, nor the time elapsed between the flow and the formation of the upper sandstone stratum.

Now suppose the geologist, looking further, finds a "double sandwich"—a sandstone stratum, a lava flow beneath it, another sandstone layer, and another flow beneath that. The flows yield the same radiometric date. Immediately the geologist knows the age of the sandstone layer between the flows—it must be the same as their age. Further, he now knows the age of the fossils in the sandstone between the flows. So, when he goes to another locality and finds similar fossils in a stratum there, he has at least an approximate age for that stratum even without a radioactivity test.

DATING MAY NOT BE EASY

Radiometric dating cannot be exact. It can be compared to measuring a distance of 100 yards with a one-foot ruler. Radiometric dates are always given, therefore, with a margin of possible error. The oldest-known rock, the Greenland gneiss, is dated at 3.76 billion ± 70 million years. The error could be 70 million years more or less.

Even if dating techniques were perfect, the rock sample might not be. Its radioactive "clock" might have been knocked out of adjustment by some event that removed emitted particles or some of the rock material. Geologists therefore like to use more than one sample, and they check dates against other available information, including relative ages of fossils or the rock strata.

Even fossils may be unreliable. Some species, such as certain trilobites, changed so little over millions of years that they can give only a very broadly approximate date. Geologists prefer a species that existed during a relatively short geologic time span in many localities. These are called index fossils. The ones that have radioactive dates are especially useful.

TELLTALE CARBON

The breakdown of uranium and certain other radioactive elements is so slow that these ele-

ments make poor measuring standards for periods of mere thousands of years. (Using uranium to measure 1,000 years would be like using a yardstick to measure a grain of sand.) Carbon-14, which breaks down to nitrogen-14 in 5,600 years, is better for the short periods.

Carbon-14 is absorbed from the atmosphere by tissues of plants and animals during life, but not after death. Therefore the stage of breakdown of carbon-14 in dead tissue indicates how long ago death occurred. The test is accurate to within about 1,000 years for periods up to 45,000 years.

Carbon-14 is used to date relatively recent geologic events. In Wisconsin, for example,

Fossils as keys to age—*The opposite outcrops here look alike. But are they? Trilobites in strata 4 and 4a are Lower Cambrian (see chart, p. 174). Fossils in 3 and 3a are Middle Cambrian, but the one in 2a is Silurian—much younger. Likewise the trilobite in 1a is Devonian, much younger than the specimen in stratum 1, which is Ordovician. Therefore the geologist decides there was a long break between 3a and 2a. The presence of the disconformity between 3a and 2a is supporting evidence.*

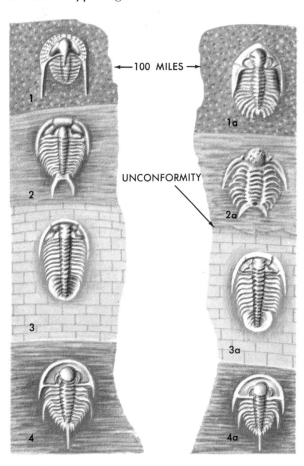

173

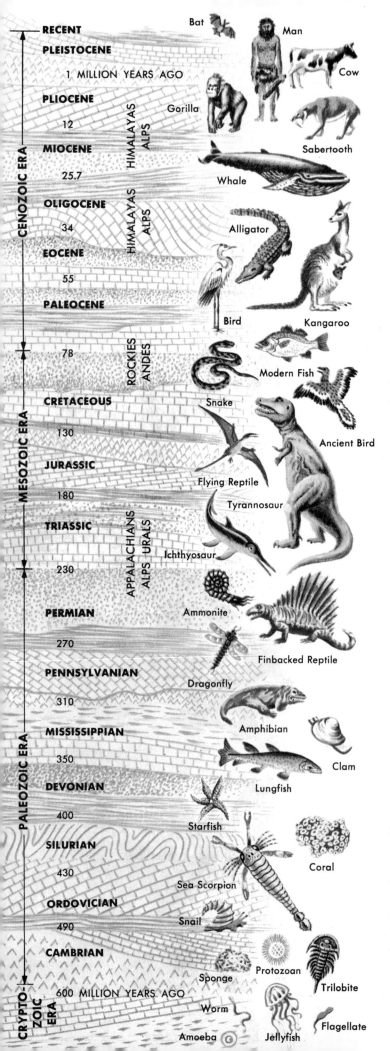

carbon-14 was tested in fossil trees that were felled and buried by advancing ice in the most recent Pleistocene glacial advance. The test gave 11,000 to 12,000 years as the time elapsed since the trees died. Other geological evidence shows that in this area the ice sheet was indeed advancing between 11,000 and 12,000 years ago.

Plant and animal ages may point to still further information. Just as in Wisconsin the tree remains dated the ice sheet, so in another place fish remains date an ancient lake, bones tell the age of a rock stratum, and trees buried under desert sands tell how long ago the region was fertile.

THE GEOLOGIC COLUMN

Earth's history is told on countless "pages" of rocks that are scattered over the globe. The pages are not numbered, there are many duplicates, many are torn and tattered, and some are missing. It is the geologist's task—and his joy— to put them in the right order and read them through.

Geology has given us a remarkably detailed, though still incomplete, record of Earth's past billion years. The record for the previous three to four billion years is still sketchy. How the planet was born, and how the lands and oceans came into being, are matters of theory. But about four billion years ago, it is thought, continents and seas did exist. By that time or shortly after, simple organisms must have lived in the ocean. Geological events since then have been rather like events changing Earth today.

As Georges Cuvier noticed, Earth history divides naturally into eras. Boundaries between these are not always clear, but each era did have its sets of typical animals and plants. Each began or ended with important geological events such as outbursts of volcanic activity, changes in climate, widespread mountain building, the sinking of some lands to become sea

The geologic column—Ages are shown from oldest (bottom) to youngest. Eras are divided by periods of major mountain-building and volcanic activity. Life evolves from the single cell to complex mammal forms. The Cenozoic Era is divided into relatively short "epochs"; other eras, into longer "periods."

bottom, and the rising of some bottoms to become land. These events changed the conditions of life, so that some old forms died out and new ones appeared.

The eras divide naturally into periods. These shorter time spans, likewise, were separated by important geological events. The list of eras and periods, with their major events and changing forms of life, is called the Geologic Column.

ALMOST TOO STRANGE TO BELIEVE

The Geologic Column gives us a bird's-eye view of the planet's history, yet it can hardly begin to suggest the enormous span of geologic time, the multitudes of living things that have come and gone, the ancient scenes that are no more. Behind the name of each single period is a history too vast for the mind to comprehend, and sometimes almost too strange for one to believe.

What are the meanings of these odd names—Cambrian and Devonian, Pennsylvanian and Jurassic, Eocene and Pleistocene? They mean sea bottoms heaving up to become Rockies, Alps, Himalayas . . . ice sheets over the Mississippi Valley, northern France and Germany, and the Congo . . . streams depositing rock waste to depths of miles . . . the roots of submarine mountains, the dark ocean trenches, preparing their earthquakes . . . Greenland and Antarctica, places of sun and waving palms . . . Wyoming, a land of swamps and dinosaurs . . . the slow, irresistible transformation of matter in the hearts of mountains . . . and, everywhere on the planet, the forms of life multiplying and struggling and finding the new forms that have led to man and his neighbors of the twentieth century—a century which is but a fraction of a second on the geological clock, whose hands still point to a morning hour.

A bridge to the past—*Natural scenery everywhere links us with remote ages of our Earth. This feature is Owachomo Bridge, in Utah's Natural Bridges National Monument.*

INDEX

(**Boldface** indicates pages on which there are illustrations related to the subjects.)

177

A